THE
WORLD
IN OUR
WORDS

The World In Our Words © 2024 by Stephanie Rowe

The moral rights of Stephanie Rowe have been identified as one of the poets who contributed to the body of work and who has the authority to publish this book. Her work is contained within this book alongside twenty-one other poets from around the globe who have submitted individually or have the authority to submit work on behalf of a family member, creating a collection of poems, and have been asserted in accordance with the Copyright Act 1968.

First published in Australia, April 2024 by Stephanie Rowe
Revised May 2024

Cover design by A.J. Haigh & Kyla Jay

Prepared for publication by Kyla Jay

ISBN: 978-0-6457693-9-5

Any opinions expressed in this work are exclusively those of each individual author and are not necessarily the views held or endorsed by the publisher.

All rights reserved. No part of this publication may be reproduced or transmitted by any means, electronic, photocopying or otherwise, without the prior written permission of the author.

WEBSITE:
www.mrsrowe.org / www.theworldinourwords.weebly.com

FACEBOOK:
Mrs Rowe Author / Poetry Page - The World In Our Words

INSTAGRAM:
Mrs_Rowe_Author

DISCLAIMER

All the information, techniques, skills and concepts contained within this publication are of the nature of general comment only and are not in any way recommended as individual advice. The intent is to offer a variety of information to provide a wider range of choices now and in the future, recognising that we all have widely diverse circumstances and viewpoints. Should any reader choose to make use of the information herein, this is their decision, and the author/s and publisher/s do not assume any responsibilities whatsoever under any conditions or circumstances. The author does not take responsibility for the business, financial, personal or other success, results or fulfilment upon the readers' decision to use this information. It is recommended that the reader obtain their own independent advice.

Note from Stephanie Rowe to the reader:

I acknowledge the first nations people of Australia, and all first nations people around the globe. I give my respect to all ancestors past and present and for future generations to walk this beautiful world.

I, Stephanie Rowe, would like to personally thank you for purchasing a book from a self-published poet. Your purchase assists artists and writers to continue doing what they love. As a collaborative project we appreciate your purchase and do not take it lightly, thank you. Thank you for supporting poets, writers, authors, and artists. Your purchase assists in the thriving of culture for humanity, we do not take your support for granted and it is deeply appreciated.

The World In Our Words poetry book is a tribute to humanity that poets from around the globe have contributed to. In a world with so much turmoil this poetry book will take you on a journey through the eyes and souls of the poets. This was my way of showing how humanity can unite through words, through poetry.

Without constraints, the poetry submitted has surpassed expectations in quality, reflecting all aspects of life, from the serious to the humorous. *The World In Our Words* is a unique project that showcases incredible poets, portraying the multifaceted nature of humanity with varying subjects and styles.

The reader will be taken on an unapologetic journey of subjects and styles of poems from around the world, with the liberty of freedom given to the poet in the submission of poetry. Expressing the highs and lows experienced within life. Allowing the poet to express themselves authentically with no restraints, a collaboration which is truly special.

One of the most unique parts of this book is it contains five different languages, pushing the conception of poets contributing but also the reader in broadening the perspective of poetry.

Some poems are in the native tongue of the poet, and some poets have been kind enough to translate their poems into English. This book contains Vietnamese, Portuguese, Spanish, Hebrew, and English.

I put a call out on social media and through my personal networks, which yielded an overwhelming response. Twenty-two (including myself) contributors from around the globe joined, covering nationalities and ethnicities spanning Israel, Scotland, England, America (including first nations peoples), Brazil, Mexico, Canada (including a Filipino-Canadian), and Australia. *The World In Our Words* has evolved into a joyous celebration of diverse voices, allowing poets to express in their native tongues and transcending boundaries.

I, Stephanie Rowe, am from Australia and other poets who have contributed to this poetry book are also from Australia. We have grown up in a country where the education system teaches us to spell certain words differently to other countries. Within saying this, we have people contributing from all around the world, which means spelling might be different depending on what poet you are reading. Please be mindful of this, we are bringing the world to your fingertips. When reading this book, you might come across some words which look a little funny. They aren't, it is just a different way of spelling.

As they say, it takes all kinds in this world.

I'd also like to request that you take a moment to rate and review this book. Please share with your friends, family, and networks Sharing will help all poets in this book sustain their passion for writing.

Yours faithfully with much love,

Stephanie Rowe

THE WORLD IN OUR WORDS

by Stephanie Rowe
includes the following contributors:

A.J. HAIGH
AZARIA CAMARGO
DAVID OLIVER
FIANNA MELODY MCDONALD
G. WIGGINS
JACQUELINE LEWIS
JANE RICHARDS
JONA ESELAYE DAVID
KYLA JAY
LUCY ALEXANDRA HOWSON
LUCY NOVARO
MARION S. LOVELAND
NATHANIEL NEW-CASTLE
NIAMH FRIEL
RANDY LACEY
RHETORICAL ARTZ
RONI ADAM
SHERR MARIE ALTAMIRANO DIAZ
SKYE PRICE
STEPHANIE ROWE
TERRICA STRUDWICK
TK CASSIDY
YANE KRITSKI DE OLIVEIRA

I would like to thank and acknowledge everyone who assisted in making this poetry book come to life.

CONTENTS

Roni Adam 12
Randy Lacey 22
Marion S. Loveland (M.E. Sloan) 34
Fianna Melody McDonald 52
Lucy Alexandra Howson (LAH) 72
David Oliver 88
Nathaniel New-Castle (N. N. Castle) 98
Lucy Novaro 112
A.J. Haigh 118
Niamh Friel 124
Jacqueline Lewis (Free) 136
Sherr Marie Altamirano Diaz (Bullet) 148
TK Cassidy 160
Yane Kritski de Oliveira 166
Kyla Jay 186
Rhetorical Artz 198
G. Wiggins 216
Azaria Camargo 224
Jona Eselaye David 234
Terrica Strudwick 240
Skye Price 252
Jane Richards 260
Stephanie Rowe (Mrs Rowe) 268
Collaborative Poem 288

RONI ADAM
ISRAEL

BIO

Born and raised in Rehovot, Israel, Roni has a master's degree in comparative literature. She was a literature teacher at high school, and is a facilitator of workshops for creative writing, therapeutic writing and reading groups.

She is a graduate of the Halikon Home for Poetry and a member of the Wednesday Group, whose members have been writing and publishing in Israel for over two decades.

Her first book, As if nothing was torn, was published In 2014 by Pardes Publishing. Her second book, But a door, was published in 2022 by Emda Publishing.

They say

They say deal with it, look it in the eyes
Into the depth of it, when it appears in a dream, name it
Write it, paint it , sculpt , dance , stomp on it with your feet
Remove the energy from it
Consult a seer who will see it in the constellation
In the unfolding cards, in the coffee grounds left at the bottom
The light will expose it.

And I say drop it, leave it, forget any trace of it
Sail through your life like tranquil lotus leaves
In the middle of a forest, waiting for a ray of sunlight
To nurture in your green heart
One floating flower.

PURE

And I already thought that it wouldn't happen
So when blood was revealed I didn't know how and why
Mother saw stains on the sheet and blanket, proudly said
"At my time no one explained or knew."

Roll the red cotton wool, wrap and bury it under the garbage
This is dirt and filth that comes out of your body
From now on you are at risk, you are Niddah*
A woman
A female, shame, shame.

And days of intense desire came
A woman, a female.
And days of cramps came, sharp pain and uncontrolled anger.
Behind my back they said, leave her, she is menstruating
And he was teasing, telling the children, let's find shelter.

At forty-five I asked the doctor
What can I use instead of birth control pills
You don't need anything
It's only a mucous discharge, you are not a fertile
female
Shame, woman's shame.

At fifty-five it came less and less
Brightened, stopped.

Now all my days are pure and nights
Not from desire
A female a woman.

*In Orthodox Judaism, a niddah is a woman during menstruation

Odian Al Hindi

Sixteen people were murdered on my street
Murder is not new to me.
When I was five years old, I went with my mother to a seamstress
She took our measurements. We didn't get dresses, she was murdered.
Each murder leads to the next.
We got used to it, the killers also got use to it, they are among us
All the time. Every day a mother watches the murderer who killed her son
Free. Anyone can murder. Maybe
I will be harmed by mistake, maybe
Deliberately. Can not
Leave. If only
My life will be safe.

Reflections on everyday death

*

I remove scales from the white flesh of fish
Mince, spice , cook
Eat a dead body in sauce.

*

Every time my eyes are caught in the nets
Of wrinkles on the faces of my friends
My end floats towards me.

*

Each morning that I wake up without the fear, the threat
She will take her own life
I am alive.

Good morning (English)

Behind me a house from which comes the aroma of baking cake
On my way, through the car window, a young father stands behind his little daughter sitting on a bench.
She holds a cookie, he arranges the ponytail on the top of her head.
A woman attracts my gaze, walking briskly while talking excitedly to a small rectangle held in her palm.
On Sadeh Road, a line of cars, the traffic jam of eight o'clock, on my right and left the cemetery is now deserted.
On the radio, the discussion starts with the interviewer saying "good morning," the interviewee replies "Amen" - in Australia no one needs a faith first thing in the morning.
The newsreader "We are allowed to publish - two soldiers were killed last night in Gaza...". Switching off, park, exit.
Taking a yoga mat from the trunk. Taking hold of myself, to breathe, to be a body for an hour.
Getting home, the phone screen lights up, an update.
The deceased today are Roy and Raz, and the hostage in the video is Noa My breath falters, my head explodes.
Suddenly a rain burst, washing away the summer dust from my windows, shining leaves all around. Joy rises in me for a second until "they are there in the war, wet to their bones, oh no"
Immediately checking the weather app, Gaza – Clear.
Only the sky.

בוקר טוב

מאחורי בית שעולה ממנו הבל אפיית עוגה
בדרך מבעד לחלון המכונית אב צעיר עומד מאחורי בתו הקטנה היושבת על ספסל
היא מכרסמת עוגיה הוא מסדר לשביעות רצונה או רצונו את הקוקו שבקדקוד ראשה.
שמנמונת חוצה את מבטי משמאל מהלכת נמרצות תוך דיבור להוט למלבּן מתכת האחוז בכף ידה.
בדרך השדה טור מכוניות של שמונה בבוקר, מימין ומשמאל בית הקברות המרכזי, שומם עתה.
ברדיו אומר בן השיח למראיין "בוקר טוב", הלה משיב "אמן" – באוסטרליה אין צורך באמונה לשם כך.
מהדורת החדשות " הותר לפרסום - שני חיילים נהרגו אמש בעזה..".
מכבה, חונה, יוצאת.
אוספת מזרן יוגה מתא המטען, את עצמי. לנשום, להיות לשעה ורבע גוף. שבתי הביתה, מסך הטלפון מאיר, עדכון.
המתים היום הם רועי ורז והחטופה נועה שנראתה בסרטון, גם, הנשימה נעתקת, הראש מתפוצץ.
אחר הצהריים – הגשם פורץ באחת, שוטף אבק קיץ מן הזגוגיות מבהיק את כל העלים סביב סביב.
שמחה עלתה בי עד להבלחה והם שם במלחמה, רטובים עד הלשד, אוי אוי בודקת מיד באפליקציה עזה – בינתיים שם שמים בהירים.

From a place no one sees

Around one bowl of food children eat with their hands
Animals, the volunteer calls them.
*

Every morning she walks ten kilometers
Barefoot with a baby on her back, and returns
On her head, twenty liters of water
Dirty, black that kills.
*

Shanita wants to learn at school
With the money, father bought
A goat.
*

Albinos hide in their houses from the sun, witchcraft and curses
Sending arrows, hunting for a limb from their white body.
By the age of thirty they are all
dead.
*

An aerial photograph

Six giraffes, lying down in a circle
Side by side, dying
The water reservoir is dry.

RANDY LACEY
CANADA

BIO

Randy was born and raised in Ottawa, but now calls central Alberta home. He has been adapting to his life as a visually impaired individual since 2011. Randy has been writing poetry since High School in Ottawa. He has self-published 12 books of poetry since 2013, and has appeared in two anthologies, Artificial Divide, and Alchemy & Miracles. He is now exploring other genres and styles with hopes of publishing in the future. When not busy writing, Randy blends spices, hot sauces, and is a content creator when he finds the spare time he's been promised.

CONTEXT FOR POEMS

The poem A Tripartite Tryst was conceived as I pondered a simple thought, a "what if" scenario, if you will. What if Me,

Myself & I had a debate about which ones more important to the being they are within?

The poem Colors of the Mind I simply put into words the answers people often ask the blind or visually impaired. Questions such as, when you dream do you see things or are you blind in your dreams? Do you see colors in your dreams? You get the idea.

Ever Been was written in the early morning of a sleepless night. Sitting on the side of my bed I asked my cat Sox if he had ever been so tired that he couldn't sleep. The rest just followed.

CONNECT
Facebook @RandytheRhymer
www.amazon.ca/stores/Randy-Lacey/author/B07TK1TPHD
www.therandylacey.ca

Colors of the Mind

In darkness, birthed a world unseen.
No hues, no shades, no trace of green
No colors painted on the mind.
Yet in the void, dreams still unwind.

What does one see without the light?
A canvas blank, a starless night
But still the mind can conjure sights.
In dreams, the blind can see the bright

Perhaps their dreams are black and white.
Or maybe they're colors which burst to life.
The mind's eye has no rules to follow.
In dreams, possibilities are not shallow.

A symphony of sounds and feels.
The rustling leaves, the spinning wheels
The scent of flowers in the air
In dreams, there's nothing one can't share.

The blind may dream of what they've heard.
A world where every sound's a word
Or maybe touch becomes a sight.
In dreams, their world is filled with light.

For what is sight but just a tool?
A way to see, a way to fool.
The mind can paint a brighter hue.
In dreams, the blind see what is true.

So, let us not assume we know.
What in their dreams they undergo
For in the darkness of their mind
A world of colors they can find.

Ever Been?

Have you ever been so tired that you couldn't sleep?
Or ever cried so much that you could no longer weep?
Have you ever been so lonely you feel empty inside?
Or ever been so frightened you just want to hide?
Have you ever been so happy you couldn't stop smiling?
Have you ever been happy?
Have you ever been?
Have you ever?
Have you?

A Tripartite Tryst

In the chambers of my mind, a conversation profound,
Between the realms of me, myself, and I, I found.
Philosophy's whispers filled the air so still,
As we pondered the existence of our collective will.

Me, the one who ventures into the world's array,
With dreams that dance in sunlight's golden ray,
Tell me, what meaning lies beyond this mortal coil?
In depths of solitude, do we find the truth and toil?

Myself, the mirror of all I've come to be,
Reflecting virtues, flaws, and shades of me,
In quiet contemplation, we seek understanding's key,
Does the essence of our being rest in unity?

I, the witness, the observer in this grand affair,
Inward and outward, exploring life's labyrinthine lair,
I am the questioner, the seeker of the profound,
Yearning for insights that resound.

Me whispers, "Existence lies in experiences sought,
In every breath, every lesson dearly bought,
Through love and laughter, pain, and strife,
We shape the tapestry of our singular life."

Myself muses, "Yet, are we not a tapestry woven,
From threads of memories, hopes, and dreams unspoken.
In our solitary moments, we navigate this vast unknown,
Drawing strength from the echoes of voices we've sown."

I interjects, "But is there not a thread that binds us tight?
An unseen force that keeps us unified, despite the fight.
For we are more than mere fragments of a whole,
Our essence intertwines, an eternal dance of soul."

And so, the conversation weaves a tapestry of thought,
A symphony of words, battles fiercely fought,
Three aspects of one being, in harmony or strife,
Exploring the depths of our existence, and the meaning of life.

Together we delve into the enigma of our being,
Seeking truth in realms unseen and freeing,
For in the depths of philosophical inquiry,
We find the essence of our unique tripartite symphony.

Oh, Me, Myself, and I, entwined in introspection,
May we forever embrace this profound connection,
And as we wander life's intricate maze,
Let us find solace in these conversations that amaze.

A Symposium of Senses

In a realm where senses converge,
A debate unfolded, with fervent urge,
Five companions gathered, each unique,
To proclaim their worth, to passionately speak.

First spoke the eyes, with vision profound,
Beholding beauty, the world's canvas unbound,
"Through me, the wonders of life unfold,
Colors and shapes, stories untold."

Next, the nose stepped forth, proud and bold,
"With fragrance and scent, my tale is told,
Aromas wafting, memories they bring,
The essence of life, a fragrant spring."

Then came the ears, attuned to sound,
"Ah, music and laughter, joys unbound,
Through me, the symphony of life resounds,
Whispers and melodies, harmonies profound."

Taste followed suit, with a delectable claim,
"On the palate's stage, I earn my fame,
Flavors and spices, a culinary delight,
Savoring sensations, day and night."

Lastly, touch spoke softly, yet with might,
"Caresses and textures, both warm and slight,
Through me, connections are deeply felt,
Embraces and sensations, where hearts are dealt."

As the debate raged, each sense defended,
Their merits proclaimed, the debate extended,
But a whisper arose, a truth to impart,
Unity they sought, not to tear apart.

For in the symphony of senses entwined,
A harmonious dance, where perceptions bind,
Each sense, a brushstroke on life's grand art,
A symphony of sensations, a masterpiece at heart.

So let us not dwell on which is supreme,
For together they form life's vibrant theme,
In unison they play, in exquisite accord,
The senses, united, in their splendor adored.

For sight, smell, hearing, taste, and touch,
Are threads of existence, a tapestry's clutch,
Enjoy them all, within each and every space
And let their symphony guide you, in life's embrace.

Sunset on the Edge of Forever

The land of the midnight sun, where darkness fears to tread,
A place of eerie beauty, where the night is never dead.
The sky, a canvas painted in hues of orange and gold,
The stars, like diamonds set in black, never to grow old.

The mountains stand like giants, silent sentinels of time,
The rivers, like veins of silver, flow with a gentle chime.
The trees, like skeletal fingers, reach towards the sky,
Their branches rustling whispers, that no one can deny.

In this land of mysteries, where shadows dance and play,
Where the sun never sets, and the night never fades away,
There's a sense of foreboding, a feeling of unease,
As if something lurks in the darkness, waiting to seize.

But still, we cannot resist the call of this haunting place,
We are drawn to its beauty, to its cold and lonely grace.
For there is something in the midnight sun that speaks to us,
A yearning for adventure, a desire to explore and trust.

So let us wander, hand in hand, through this strange and wondrous land,
Let us embrace the mystery, the beauty that's at hand.
For in the land of the midnight sun, there's magic to be found,
And though we may be lost, we are never truly bound.

The Pursuit of Imperfection

Nothing I can say or do will ever be right.
There's nothing I can ever do in your sight.
To make things better, to make things right,

Embracing imperfections, I find my grace,
In the flawed moments, my soul finds its place.
For perfection's pursuit, an endless race,
I'll let go, surrender, and set my own pace.

In each stumble and fall, I'll find my way,
To unfold the beauty of life's disarray.
For it's within the cracks that light will play,
With this imperfect masterpiece, day by day.

No longer confined by judgment's cruel sting,
I'll dance with flaws and let my spirit sing.
In the pursuit of imperfection, my offering
Authenticity is the gift I shall bring.

For perfection is a myth, a hollow ,
True beauty lies in the imperfect gleam.
So, with open arms, I'll embrace the stream,
And find solace in life's imperfect theme.

Yes, if wrong is the best that I can ever do,
Then that's the rightest I can be for you,

No One to Blame...But Me

I have had my share of troubles
Of this there can be no doubt
But through it all, I kept my head high
Never let myself dwell in self-pity's clout

I stumbled upon rocky roads
Yet, I never gave up the fight
For I knew deep within my soul
That strength would guide me towards the light

The storms may rage, fierce and wild
But I'll weather them, come what may
With resilience as my trusted shield
I'll overcome, I'll find my way

For every failure that I've faced
I've learned and grown, my spirit ablaze
No one to blame, but me alone
In my hands, my destiny lays

I'll rise from the ashes, phoenix strong
And write a tale of my own design
Through perseverance and sheer will
I'll sculpt a future that will truly shine

No need for excuses or pointing fingers
The choices I make shape my destiny
So I'll embrace each challenge that lingers
With open arms, I'll set myself free

In this journey of life, I'll find my flame
Illuminate paths where dreams can be
With courage as my unwavering name
The architect of my own reality... is me

MARION S. LOVELAND
(1908 - 2006)
UNITED STATES OF AMERICA

BIO

My grandmother, Marion Sloan Loveland, (pen name M.E. Sloan) was born in Newburg, New York on June 14, 1908. She graduated from the University of New York at Albany and taught high school English before moving to Vermont. She was a member of the American Association of University Women, Friends in Council, the Home Study Club, the Vermont Historical Society, the Union Book Club, and volunteered extensively in church, school and community activities.

At age 89, the College of St. Joseph the Provider in Rutland, Vermont, awarded her an Honorary Doctorate of Humanities. Grandma Loveland was an avid reader and an accomplished poet. Although never formally published, she was a prolific composer of prose and loved to share her writing with others. I am proud to be able to share some of her work posthumously in this wonderful collection; I know she would be honoured.

- Kim Loveland Bruce (granddaughter)

RICH MAN, BEGGAR MAN

Oh, once I met a beggar man
while touring Dublin town.
Because he seemed so cheerful
beside him I sat down.

When we had talked a while
I found his philosophy
had made him happily content,
and proved the beggar, me.

He'd known well beauty of this earth
and warmth of friends, but I
who'd travelled far in search of both,
found they had passed me by.

CULTIVATE HAPPINESS

Tucked in the corners of my mind,
are many memories.
Some sad, some glad, some painful, too,
but all a part of me.

The secret of a wondrous life
that makes you feel secure,
is to cultivate the happy times,
use bad ones for manure.

GRANDPARENTS
God did very well with the sun and the moon
With the planets and stars up above;
But one of his best inventions, I think,
Are Grandmas and Grandpas to love.

COBWEBS ON THE BROOM

Dishes on the table,
dust in every room.
Lots of clothes to launder
Cobwebs on the broom.

Menus to be planned yet
Babies to be tended
So much mending to be done –
Guess my poem's ended.

DANDELIONS
As many short-stemmed drooping flowers
Two baby hands can hold,
But to mother much more precious
Than the rainbow's pot of gold.

OVERSIGHT
The sky's like an old, old curtain
Between Heaven and earth, you know;
The little stars are just the holes
small angels forgot to sew.

THE GREATEST OF THESE – FOR MY CHILDREN

With child-like trust you've asked me
to tell you what is love.
True love, my dear, is infinite –
like countless stars above.

It's kindness, understanding,
and patience without end.
It's tenderness, devotion, and a
fierceness to defend.

It's loyalty, humility and gladness
great or small;
A protection and a guidance
of weak ones who might fall.

Tranquillity of spirit and abiding
joy as well,
mark those who've found the secret,
and deep in love do dwell.

Love is seeking and it's finding
beauty all the way;
It's restless creativity,
Stirring night and day.

Either giving or receiving
benevolence or toll -
Creates peace and inward quiet
of body, mind and soul.

Throughout life, love is a sturdy staff,
it's also life's stern rod.
Perhaps you'd better understand
if I said, "Love is God."

WORDS
Words! Words are such awesome and powerful things.
Some are fragile as butterfly wings;
Some are uplifting, so joyful and gay,
lilting like laughter of children at play.
Others are sharp like a steel blade honed keen,
cutting the heart and scraping it clean
of love.

THROUGH THE VALLEY

Why does fear clutch at a small child's heart
when he's put to bed at night?
Why must he have a Teddy to hold-
the assurance of a light?

Like you and me, he fears the unknown,
It is not the dark of night.
A hand to hold, or some cuddly thing
Makes everything seem all right.

Hold him quite close and sing him a song,
But teach him the faith he needs.
Soon he will be out of your arms, and then
his faith he'll express in deeds.

Give him your love and smile away fears.
Then put his hand in God's own.
Though the journey's long and his feet are small,
He need never walk alone.

PROBLEM SOLVING

When you have problems to be solved
Write lists – 1, 2 and 3.
Answers to questions on line one are YES,
simple as can be.

In the second category,
the answers will be NO
That seems a good solution when
You're "going with the flow".

The third list is my favorite
A catch-all, as you can see
This list is just "The hell with it"
Or category 3.

HIGH TEA IN ARDAUGH
Plain food on a rough-hewn table,
Fresh-scrubbed, but grooved by wear.
Strong tea, sliced ham, potato bread;
her bounty, spread with care.

We had not eaten since morning
and far afield had roamed;
lured by enchanting lake and glen,
we'd roved the hills of home.

As the sun went down, strength faded
and we felt our weariness.
Tired earth, not quite possessed by night
betrayed grey eeriness.

A golden halo of lamplight
lit a window along the way,
and a head bowed over work-worn hands
telling deeds at end of day.

To intrude on such devotion
seemed impious sacrilege.
But she had sensed our coming,
for when we passed the hedge,

she stood by the lighted doorway,
and her heart, 'twas open wide.
The warmth of her greeting cheered us –
"Share a bit o' God's love inside?"

TRY IT FOR SIZE
How very quickly we forget
the burdens children bear.
The long, long paths that they must tread
For us are just a step ahead.
No wonder that they often think
perhaps we do not care.

Before you give a little child
a task that he must do
Sit down upon his little chair
to get his point of view.
Imagine you're his size and age –
How does it seem to you?

TEA LEAVES

My mother was an artist,
without palette, paint or brush.
Her best sketches were not charcoal, but
drawn with love and trust.

She always saw the best in folks,
and subtly drew them out,
Until they quite forgot themselves,
and lost their fears and doubt.

Whenever someone came to call,
she'd make a cup of tea.
And no one guessed its secret blend
was kindness and sympathy.

Her cookies, cakes or home-made bread
were served with grace and care.
The best ingredients she used –
True thankfulness and prayer.

As teacups gaily rattled
and talk prompted by her cheer
became very light and happy,
You would realize how dear

she was, and why we loved her so.
Then came the magic hour
in which the tea-leaves she would read!
We all believed her power;

She must have had some inner sight
 for always she could see -
not what was patently revealed,
but what each soul could be.

SELF PRESERVATION
An old friend who came to call on me
said, "My, you are well preserved."
I didn't know what he meant by that –
or, if it was well-deserved.

At my age, nice compliments are few
They never flow, just trickle.
As I pondered this, I asked myself –
"Am I canned, freeze-dried, or pickled?"

GARDEN OF DREAMS
Her garden – in a year or two -
Would be all that she had dreamed.
Blue larkspur- tall for background
And pink hollyhocks, it seemed,
Would help recall the flowers that
Mother had raised and loved –
Alyssum, lilies, rosemary and hight bells of foxglove.

There should be purple lilac trees,
And rambler roses red.
Perennials she had well-planned; for
cutting, one large bed.
To dream this fragrant garden was
an overflowing cup!

Meanwhile –
she watered pansies in her window - six flights up.

HERITAGE
To hear wood thrush sing at sunset's glow,
To find arbutus bursting through the snow,
To see fir trees hushed by snow silence,
To walk through woodlands unspoiled by barbed fence or wall;
To seek and find fulfillment in beauty,
To feel God's presence and His love so free,
To walk alone, but never lonely be.

To me, these seem the grandest heritage of all.

FIANNA MELODY MCDONALD
AUSTRALIA

BIO

Meet Fianna McDonald, a 32-year-old Australian mother of two, currently residing in rural Victoria. Her life's journey, marked by a teenage move across the world for love, has become the foundation of her poetic exploration. Navigating 13 years of marriage and parenting neurodivergent children, Fianna has found solace in writing amidst the challenges of chronic illness, late-diagnosed neurodiversity, and PTSD from being witness and first responder to a fatal road accident.

From her childhood she has cherished the written word, engaging in both poetry and story writing, and now, her contribution to this poetry publication unveils a narrative of self-discovery, resilience, and the pursuit of a healed self and community.

Writing has been a lifelong companion for Fianna, offering a safe haven where she can explore all aspects of herself and her experiences. Most recently this has been in the form of spoken word poetry, inspired and introduced by fellow contributor and friend Rhetorical Artz, into weaving words with showmanship and vocal expression. Videos of such pieces will become available on her social media platforms mentioned below.

Beyond this initial publication, Fianna has also begun crafting a children's picture book series and her debut fantasy novel, reflecting her commitment to the author she always was and the boundless possibilities of her imagination.

CONTEXT FOR POEMS
Through her free form verses, Fianna invites readers to join her on a journey of liberation and interconnection, each poem a testament to the transformative power of words and their many meanings, and the unfolding tapestry of life's experiences and emotions.

CONNECT
TikTok @melodyesque
Facebook @Melodyesque Muses

A Philosophy of Life

I've been meditating recently.
Letting thoughts evaporate as internal spaces consume me.
I stopped telling myself I couldn't and just allowed myself to suck at it in the beginning.
Riding mental waves while I try to draw that energy up inside of me.
I've been *believing* lately.
Believing that my mind might not have always known what was best for me.
Conditioned to survive, but not unwinding till I thrive.
I've been questioning the state of things,
Existential crises have been knocking at the core of me.

Did you know that they've now proven that our minds tell our eyes what to see,
instead of just applying meaning to the images they receive?
Nothing could convince me more;
I'm a living, breathing processor for an experience simulator.
'Divinity', just a contraction for 'dive into unity'.
The best parts of us were meant to reflect that diversity.
The message got lost when they tried to tell us the divine was far above,
preached that we were flawed and shamed us with what they taught.
Made _GOD_ into everything that wasn't us,
while they used *our very Godliness* to further break us all apart.
A thousand years of trauma
A thousand more of loss
but the collective keeps collecting for each experience is raindrops forming clouds above.

We've made a hundred different mirrors without really seeing what reflects in them.
Our brains were designed to process our experience of time.

We keep ourselves switched on autopilot then complain that we can't drive.
So, keep asking 'Why?'
even if it looks like the end of the alphabet has been reached.
Like breaking down an atom just to see what it could teach.
We think our lives are normal when there's still parts of us
they couldn't break apart enough to reach.
Just a bunch of empty space vibrating to different frequencies.

When I judge you, I judge the hidden parts of me.
When I love you, I allow myself to shine with the radiance of everything.
I apply energy to the words to find they've twisted all their meaning,
Suddenly 'reality' is a reflection of the feelings I've been conducting.
'Re' is to do again; back to the origin,
'al' is pertaining to, 'ity' is the condition or quality of what it's tied to.
So read this back and get;
'What is real for you just pertains to the quality, or condition,
of how you get back to your origin, or beginning.'
There's spirals of knowledge and levels to unlock it in.
Laugh, for we've only just stepped from the tutorial zone we've been living.

Stop.
Flip the code and question what is motivating.
Am I really overcome or just, suddenly aware of what came over me?
For One to become m a n y it had to create form and feelings.
To identify each self for itself, a firewall was made to protect our sense of identity.
So we might experience separation, isolation, and apply meaning to things divisively.
So we might experience ourselves from each of our own refractories.

This firewall filters how my mind processes reality.
It is the ego that allows me to be me, independently.
What if we forgot more than just what we are?
What if every moment we wish to wake up, we do so?
But to be present here, there can be no recollection of a dimension that is made of everything outside, inside, and around, of this one.

Just something I ponder, never sure where I'll land -
For how could a mortal construct understand?
Like how could a computer run a program made for technology far more advanced?
But here we are.
So the journey must be important enough to step back into this experience.
Perhaps only in the sense that we take it,
not in how, or what path, or that it shouldn't feel overwhelming or inadequate in the face of how quickly it all seems to fall apart again.
If we did wake up... then we do keep diving back.
This is all part of Divinity experiencing material limitations.
So trust your heart
Explore **every** part
and come back home to collective unconditional love.

****

Sign Reader

I didn't want to be a sign reader, yet the signs kept getting read.
I tried to be illiterate, so ignorance could bless me bliss
but they kept on growing bigger and got louder and unrolled lists
and I kept on ticking boxes as I tripped between the lines.
Absorbing knowledge unknowingly until, one day, I find...
I knew what every sign had said,
every message I had tried to miss,
and now, oh no, I knew what lay just up ahead.
Hold me bound by honesty... the dread, the dread.

They'd been telling me things for years that I didn't want to know.
Then it aligned. The pattern bared.
The signs they warned;
'If you stand when you should fall,
We'll bring this fire. We'll burn your core.
You have to play the game without ruleset or board,
You'll have to stay and master harder things than words have
ever taught.'
I saw then a greater pattern to all the red strings
a conspiracy of connections;
mapped out like a language you once read
familiar but infuriatingly, no longer making any sense.

Another will leave after carving out their right to space in your heart.
Another empty chamber, filled with magma, buried after.
Is it just loss, I'm meant to master?
To remain soft, to keep my gentle.
To keep burning bright, with each growing disaster.
To pave a way, or just inspire adventure.
To learn exactly what I don't want to do to another...
While I am cut and hit and sundered.
Where I bear the load and belittle my task master.
Where I raise the whip, and I break my own heart after.

Where I refuse to drift, and keep giving out pieces when I should have quit.
Till dust and I part- where the '-icles' are nothings.
Just atoms in structures that suddenly lost all their meaning.

I don't know how to speak without seeing what lands,
like droplets of understanding that splatter unseemly.
Right in the eye - They get it! They see!
Then that one off target, or wiped off with a sleeve.
How to have conversations, when every other word
might as well be a calling card for the signs I've ignored?
Keep giving bigger chunks just to unsee what I find,
Till I can give no longer; I've given even my eyes!
I've given even my eyes.
I think I'd rather be blind.

****

Spinning Top

I'm scared one day I won't come back from the land I dissociate to, or that this slow progression is what dementia's onset feels like. Just each day losing parts of your mind to realms that your body can't follow or find.

I know the reasoning's, grasp at patches in the quilt of understanding.
Was this the trauma of a world I misaligned with or
the injuries of a soul shoved into a body misaligned with it?
Like a wild animal placed in a cage then made to call it home.
Comfort and safety, always assured, and driven all the madder for it.

Sometimes it's like I've been superimposed over this flesh.
Fighting through shadows to pull strings to control all the different aspects…
While others just move their limbs.

Where would I find words if they were touches?
Could I seek comfort in the folds of skin I've only ever been taught to hide from?
What if I run out of time, like a spinning top losing momentum;
I'm sure it too thought it would continue, as it had in the beginning.
You never really know how much energy it takes to live until you're already spinning.

****

Why are we friends?

Because the first time you smiled at me
I realized I had never heard the sunrise sing before that moment.
Because there are frequencies when we speak
that spark universes into being
and call home the parts of our soul that linger in limbo.
Because when we unravel with each other;
the loose threads just coil onto the others spool,
for safekeeping or keeping the space
we knit with needles forged
from shared experience but reflected perspectives.

Because in every story I've ever read about magic
and believing in something more,
I've found your name whispered.
Because you speak the same sentiments preached
by gurus, heroes and ancient prophets,
all in half-asleep pillow talk.
Because you taste like the warm comfort
of the campfire as the night falls,
joyful glee and the very essence of creativity.
Dancing in the ways the flames reach
 for the sun's of other galaxies.
Wistful but not despairing,
when sometimes they remain out of reach.

Because when our energies collide I deeply align
with Aladdin and Jasmine on their magic carpet ride.
Adventure, trust, and being open to all possibilities.
Together our story transcends paper and pen
and any boundaries dictated by this dimension.
Because the magic is easier to cast when
we use the focus of each other's hearts.
Because I knew you before I knew myself,

and in loving all of you
I've welcomed home some of my best parts.
Because everything makes more sense
when our energies overlap,
perfectly filling in the others gaps,
supporting exchange and mutual aid.
Where not a single block of foundation is formed with shame.

****

Love in Pieces

I'll love you to pieces,
in that I'll love you down,
to those tiny fragments of self
you might not have found.
Afraid to fit into the spaces they've left
because of society's identity theft.

I'll love your pieces;
each crumbling moment of reconstruction,
each messy milestone of self induction.
I love your segments in sequence,
till you have made peace
with the melody leading to such an orchestral feast.

I love the pieces you are still growing into,
when you count each star in your inner constellation
and understand they're all sun's with the right magnification.

I'll love the peace that you fought a hundred wars
and died a thousand times
just to love yourself enough to find.
Now instead of hurting-
you're holding yourself.
Growing out of the shit you learned to fertilize.

I love you to pieces;
I'll learn the taste of your soul,
love the places you've gone
and going to go.
But I'll love it so,
when our journey needs me to take a step back
I'll be letting you go, while my love remains intact.

I love learning how to love, without possession or rumination.
Loved getting hurt while I learnt how to manage expectations.
We should love in pieces, till we understand more of the whole.
For isn't love with conditions, just mental control?

I'll love without reason,
I'll love as I walk away.
I'll love till it's hurting,
then love you more than yesterday.
I might question this process,
some days might seem hard.
But I understand now that-
I don't love to be *comfortable*,
I love to be **loud**.

I want to be heard for the way I connect,
I want to be known for the ways I respect.
I might not fit these moulds,
I might watercolour this grey scale of canvas folds.
For when I enter a story line; the plot starts picking up pace.
Allow it the autonomy to question its state.
I might be the martyr
I might be the villain
I might be the muse that convinced you to start living!

I'll love your pieces and the whole they create
when **you** take the time to love what they make.
I might be a beacon
I might herald change
but I've learned to accept how my worth is *not* made.
I can be me.
I can love unconditionally
can honour the pieces
while I piece together my symphony.

But this music I make isn't meant to be whole...
It's part of a narrative that's sung between souls.

****

Life sentence

I am a life sentence.
Whether I feature for years in your mindscape
or just a smiling face that caught your passing eye.

I will remain.

Long after the warmth I cultivated within you fades
Long after the memory becomes dream like in its age

You can find me within.

Find me offering philosophies to your hidden strengths
Find me humming in the hollowness you tried to hide
Filling emptiness with echoes of other lives.

I am a life sentence you do not choose
I am a blessing and a curse entwined
I am the light that guides,
through the darkness created
when it flared directly into our eyes.

I am comfort to the blind.
I am comfortable being blind.
I have struggled to make sense of shadows
then realized I am a radio trying to project light.

I am not meant to be visual.

I am what remains when overwhelm subsides.
When the shapes behind closed lids start to redefine.
I am a self fulfilling prophecy;
in that I will fulfill the self that prophesied me.
I make sense of life through vibrations and sensations

words were never meant to describe.

I am a life sentence.
In that I will speak life into sentences in a language
that will be spoken long after my time.
Even as we unwind, I remain.
Even as you close your eyes, I remain.
Take a deep breath, in the unspoken seconds you hold in
I am easy to find.

I am a life sentence,
sentenced to the parts of us
that never had the chance
to be structured with the sense of us.
  Welcome me or riot.
    Herald me or quiet.
      I will remain, in **scream** or *silence*.

    ****

Decolonise and Dismantle

Written in protest to the violence that has been experienced and continues to be experienced in many places by many different people for the benefit of few. As the current death toll grows in Palestine, Sudan, the Democratic Republic of Congo and many other places where resources and land have been given more value then human life and suffering - so too does the blood on all our hands. May we bear witness to their loss and not let those responsible remain in power over us all.

Call me home to where my thoughts once roamed,
Confident in the structures they had flowed around.
Call me home to where the world seemed a safe place to rest;
Where children heard lullabies in bed, not explosions of death.

Where we might honour the natural beauty in each experience, separate and collective
And laugh at those who pedestalled conquest and imperialists.
I condemn the governments and authorities that would speak for me,

My people don't turn a blind eye to apartheid and genocide.

My people aren't limited by the countries we were born in and swore loyalty to,

Before we were old enough to know the atrocities they hid from view.
I gave no consent to having comfort while others bled and knew only hatred and death.

I walked with confident steps on land I thought I understood, thought I knew the origins of.
I kept history close, told to me from pages soaked in disrespect

And wondered what gave off such a stench while also making little sense.
I finally shelved those books that spoke with an oppressors false narrative,

Colonised and complacent, unaware and defensive.

I listened to the land instead.
Cried with her on life watered with innocent blood shed.
Sought the first caretakers and cared for how they'd been mistreated.
Added tears to the oceans of grief;

Both grateful and guilty that I don't know the horror of picking literal pieces of my family up,
Blown into a gruesome puzzle by someone else's greed and lack of humanity.
Someone that they would likely never know or meet.

Who will never walk the streets lined with their victims, most still just children.
Who force those they oppress to meet their violence with violence, for all peaceful protests are met with the hail of gunfire and more death.

I unpack the school bag given to me with teachings of privilege and greed.
Unpack the conditioning, daily, that they would have me believe.
To divide. To weaken. To control the flow of currency I no longer place such worth in.

We have always been **One** and the ways we harm each other reflect a cycle begging to be, broken.

If we'd only just listen.

We weren't the ones to start this divide of nationality and physicality, beliefs and ability.
But we are the ones who now walk this land, inherit the systems and the poison they pump, back into our hands.

We were told we had to drink because every source of water is now poisoned
and so long as we are hydrated (and sickened), we could become something better.
But we *can* survive without, until all of these water ways are cleaned.
Until all rivers and seas flow free; until all beings know safety and peace.

All it takes is allowing ourselves to feel even just a little bit thirsty, honour the discomfort in reflecting on what the price of our comfort really is and has been.
There is no us OR them, no you OR me.

We are as much each other as we all bleed and breathe.
Together we have everything we could ever need.

But we aren't free until we are all free.

****

Safe Harbour from Storming Seas

I can feel their little minds reaching as they patter up the hall,
like how their arms would speak when they were small.
Wishing to be lifted to where they find home in my hold,
held so safely their system settles so they might yet again be bold.
How beautiful to be needed like how the sun ray needs the sun...
How special is it that they find safety where we would once
have run?

And Yes, it's overwhelming when the world is hard and fast-
and we must carve a windbreak for them out of our very heart.
When in every effort to keep them safe we must name the dangers,
in the harbour that we sailed from when we were still just strangers,
to the hardships and indoctrination passed down through
generations,
that society dressed up as normal so we wouldn't question
such harmful expectations.
That the storms we cast our wills upon were ones our
parents couldn't...
and that inside us, a child remains, still wounded from being
left out in it.
One day we lift our heads from repairing shredded sails and
splintered wood,
to find a world flooded with adults still floating by on rafts made
in childhood.

Oh I can feel her wonder at what the world might be,
If she had known the shelter that my children constantly seek.
Honour that she is overwhelmed to have to share these
ravaged coves,
with other budding vessels that haven't weathered storms or foes.
That she learnt to find safety in the drenching storming emotions,
but now must find a way to model healthy regulation.

Yes make safe these shores, for children now and of our past,
Contain their storms, show them (and us) it doesn't last.
Learn how to fail, how to breathe, how to set boundaries, how to fall,
Learn how to accept what we can't control and love through it all,
I have heard it always said, how the time would seem to pass,
That we would wish to go back and find new ways to make it last.
That we will miss this once they are grown, but how,
do we be present and not miss this in the now?

Yes, deeply, I can feel their little minds reaching,
feel their little hearts beating,
feel how their love both builds me up and brings me undone.
Like how the sun ray lights up a world but still needs to be nurtured by the Sun.

****

LUCY ALEXANDRA HOWSON

(LAH)

ENGLAND, UK

BIO

Lucy Alexandra Howson, a creative spirit and dedicated mother, hails from the shire of Nottingham, UK. Her artistic journey is woven with the threads of diverse cultures and the wisdom garnered from a decade immersed in the tapestry of Vietnamese life.

In her role as both a creative soul and a nurturing mother, Lucy Alexandra Howson weaves a narrative of unity and interconnectedness, encouraging us all to walk together harmoniously on the intricate path of life.

CONTEXT FOR POEMS
Love is. Won a prize for a Buddhist poetry competition during lockdown in 2020. Translated by Nguyệt Lieu.

CONNECT
Instagram @lahvaart

For other creative endeavours:
www.behance.net/812studiovn

Love is.

Written 2020 during the pandemic while living in Vietnam and won a prize in a poetry competition run by a Buddhist organisation. Vietnamese translation follows on completed by a wonderful woman called Nguyệt Moon Lieu.

Love is Learning to smile with your eyes because your face is hidden behind a mask.

Love is Watching the clouds in sun and in storms and feeling grateful that your lungs are clean.

Love is Looking down into the rice sack and wondering how many grains we still have, yet being thankful the bag is half full.

Love is Sharing food with your neighbours so they have enough for tomorrow and not just today. So the children can have cake, and sweetness while they're stuck inside so long.

Love is phone calls with elderly loved ones, telling all that is in our heart and the hope they will stay healthy and happy for a hundred years, hoping we can see them once again.

Love is being in the moment, watching the candle flame dance and shadows flicker over our ancestors on the altar as we pray to understand the lessons the universe is teaching us.

Love is breathing in and out, and giving our souls moments of peace. Listening to the wind chimes in the afternoon sun, and gazing down to the lonely streets below.

Love makes our hearts grow stronger
Absence makes our hearts grow fonder
Love is hope for the future when the street sweepers rise to

the aroma of street coffee, Chickens crowing in the blue morning light and golden streams of sunlight creating pools of warm as the motorbikes weave between them on their way to work.

Love is the morning rush of happy children to school, parents to work, the builders to build, the monks to meditate, the artists to paint, the vendors to call out to customers, the musicians can once again play and the joy of Vietnam can begin again with a new soul of gratitude for the love we have of being alive and breathing life, once again.

Love is hope.

Tình yêu thương lúc này là
Yêu thương lúc này là những nụ cười bằng mắt
vì khuôn mặt của bạn đã bị che phía sau khẩu trang.

Yêu thương lúc này là ngắm nhìn những áng mây
và mặt trời trong cơn mưa bão và cảm thấy biết ơn
rằng phổi mình vẫn còn trong sạch.

Yêu thương bây giờ là nhìn vào
hủ gạo và tự hỏi còn bao nhiêu gạo
nữa đây và biết ơn
gạo vẫn còn một nửa.

Tình thương bây giờ là chia sẻ thức ăn với hàng xóm
để cho họ có đủ ăn vào ngày mai mà không phải chỉ có hôm nay.

Đồng thời trẻ em cũng có bánh kẹo
trong khi chúng bị giữ ở trong nhà quá lâu.

Yêu thương lúc này là những cuộc điện thoại
của những người thân cao tuổi từ xa nói rằng tất cả những gì
trong tim

họ bây giờ là hy vọng
sẽ sống vui khỏe đến hàng trăm tuổi để mong rằng sẽ có ngày gặp lại chúng tôi.

Tình yêu lúc này là những khoảnh khắc ngắm nhìn những ngọn nến lung linh cùng những hình ảnh Tổ Tiên trên bàn thờ khi cầu nguyện để hiểu rằng vũ trụ đang dạy bảo chúng ta.

Tình yêu hiện tại là việc hít thở ra vào để tâm
trí có những phút giây bình an.
Lắng nghe tiếng gió thoảng dưới ánh
nắng chiều và liếc nhìn những đường phố vắng lặng của Saigon.

Tình yêu làm tim chúng ta đập nhanh hơn.
Sự vắng mặt làm tim chúng ta thương xót hơn.

Tình yêu lúc này là niềm hy vọng cho ngày mai đường phố uốn lượn sẽ thức dậy
trải dài đến những góc phố thơm mùi cà phê.

Những chú gà gáy vào buổi sáng sớm dưới ánh nắng
của bầu trời xanh và những
dòng suối vàng của ánh mặt trời
làm nên những hồ bơi
ấm áp khi những chiếc xe máy
len lỏi giữa chúng trên đường đi làm.

Tình yêu ấy là những buổi sáng trẻ em hối hả đến trường,
cha mẹ đi làm,
những người thợ xây nhà,
những vị tu sĩ thiền định,
những nghệ nhân họa vẽ,
những người bán hàng rong kêu rao mời gọi khách hàng,
người nhạc sĩ trở lại chơi đàn.

Niềm vui của Việt Nam
sẽ bắt đầu trở lại với một linh hồn mới vừa trải qua một giai đoạn
vì tình yêu
nhân loại của chúng ta, đó là chính là việc chúng ta còn sống sót
và một lần nữa sự sống hít thở lại trở về.

Tình yêu
là hy vọng.
Tôi yêu bạn

Home

Ah to be home,
Is to never feel quite so alone
Walking accompanied by memories
Expanding like the rings on trees.

And as I watch the sun go down
By the lake in my home town
The place where I am always known
From a tiny person I have grown

In confidence.
Through baby steps
This is where my heart first leapt.
This is where I lost my innocence.

The crows quietly bumble round the lake
Humbly they bow to the orb so great
Each step I take
I vow, I will not break.

I cast my eyes to the bluest skies
The moon bright and awake
Like a mirrored earth
Celestial birth.

With the fading sunlight still warm upon my skin
I feel the evening beckoning.
I'm humbled by vast fields of green
With Deer and crows painted on this scene.

Each life so strange in its effect
So fragile, small and delicate.

I feel loved in this park.

I watch each wingspan glide upon
The air o'er blazing Wollaton Lake
My breath away this sight will always take!
So comforting is natures glow
As I rest upon the stump below.

I better move my hollow legs
Before the dusk reaches the hall
Bodies depart in their quiet flow
And back to my home I'll slowly go.

Peace I carry within my chest
And smiles for this afternoon's happy quest
Home is where I'll keep my heart
No matter where I will depart.

Memories of a Mermaid.

I sang a song for you
Beneath the blue twirling lights
Two summers ago

With closed eyes I sang that I'd fly away
Because my soul didn't know where it belonged.
And you responded
By singing a song

Telling me
To expect the worst of you.
Followed by the song my daughter was named after,
Written back in April 1970.
The same month you died fifty years later.

In that night illuminated by the twinkling fragmented disco ball
That cascaded stars against the wall,
Upon smiles of friends lounging on sofas grinning silly drunken grins,
Listening to your sweet voice as you sipped beer the entire time,
And on a chair you swivelled gently in time with the sing.

No one expected the worst of you.
We never thought
You would jump
And become lines in queer poetry
In the same space you sang those songs two summers ago.

Tonight,
Our friends silhouettes
Line the walls of the same space we shared.
The living art
Of the living room

A noise artist played loud sounds
visuals clashing playfully over the elements.
It was too much for me.
I had to step outside to calm my mind
The patterns of the music were so empty
While my interior was so full of thought.

Of you

And your sweet shadow that no longer has a chance to be divine.
The only piece of you left behind
Was the tree you made with fabric stabbed through by branches.
The fruits of your labour,

Now painfully literal.
An installation kept close to us all
But hidden
Behind a scarlet velvet curtain
To keep all the memories from spilling out.
You were the lump in my throat tonight,
And also the loudest laugh that rumbled inside my belly dancing
all the way out of my mouth.

You still make me feel things
Even though you're not around.
I still carry the weight of your decisions

In waves of guilt

For not catching you

As you leapt
And let go
Leaving everything behind you
Black.

In blueberry circles of unrest
Because you left us without answers that no amount of sleep
or searching I can find.
I never knew how much anger came with grieving,
And the creeping feeling of knowing

Accountability was not taken
By those who held the golden ticket to
Living a better life
In this realm,
And not heaven.

To someone plagued with demons
I only wish they'd listened.
You deserved to be loved.
You deserved to be helped.
You deserved to be listened to.

Only in art now can you still live on.

It hurts to still miss you,
To smell your scent in the strangest of places
The same washing powder brand I never knew the name of.
And in the aroma of the blue coffee that filled the studio in
the mornings.

I see your art in the brush strokes of other painters canvasses.
I feel your spirit
In the places we held hands

And walked with mirrored smiles
A summer of fruits so sweet
Until it went so sour.
That the entire basket was doomed to rot.

And I really did get the worst of you.
And I did indeed fly away too,
To find home in myself again.
I find myself visiting those places
We walked together
And felt happiness.
All the anger melted away after I visited you in the pagoda
And took you flowers and fruits

To try and undo the past and send you love in the afterlife.
Looking at your picture on the altar so adored,
Wishing you could have received this much loving care while your body was atoms instead of ashes.

I hope others can still enjoy the fruits of your art long into the future.
Such a chasm of wonder to behold.
The world needs you as an example of
Abstract expressionism

And as a warning to not abandon the seeds sowed within fragile minds full of storm clouds.

To remind them to water those saplings with happiness
So they can continue to grow
For many summers to come.
I wish I'd known to tell you all of these things,
Before you flew and were gone.

1,242 Days of Motherhood.

I see you growing up
Full of endless love
With quiet grace
And stubbornness
That elephant stomp
And challenges,
You're such a little woman now.
It makes me sad
For I barely had to blink
From the womb
To the breast
To that child
In my eyes
You're absolutely everything.
You're growing up so fast,
Next thing I know you'll be up to my chin,
Today you're waist height,
And can tie your shoes,
It's actually frightening.
How time passes
Without a care,
Never letting up.
Like your determination,
Those frozen moments of frustration,
Always giving way to waves of happy reckoning.
The joy of overcoming fear
And living in the now
Is something to my life you bring.

I'm so grateful
For your love.
And your morning cuddles on the mezzanine.
When you brush your teeth yourself,

Or eat all your food in your dish.
And give me hugs when I can't dream.
I'm thankful for your dad.
And that we shotgun wedding'd in the park.
That he is always there as a mellow soundtrack,
Through the light and through the dark.
Every day you make me proud.
Even when you drive mummy crazy,
You're allowed to make your own mistakes,
Even when the world is deafening,
You have to learn each thing in your own way.
So happy woman's day,
To the girl who saved my life
By changing the way I see the world,
In every level of reality.
To become the best version of a woman I can be.
Even in moments of anxiety and strife.
I love you my little woman.
Grow with courage, Like the lotus in the mud.
Persevere,
Make art and memories,
let your golden heart always glow,
And dance and sing
And be kind
And dear
And bold
And opinionated
And weird
And yourself.
Write your story In your smile,
And let your soul
Be free.

The silent scream of the feminine.

Written for a women's day event in 2014.

Don't treat me like a mannequin,
with glossy-coated plastic skin.
It's the the statue of liberty,
Got turned into an icon of feminine pornography.

She's flaking, she's shaking, her cracks visible publicly,
Iron tears fall beneath the smoggy sky, trapped within.
A businessman sees her as perfection, but,
Close up she's breathing in with endless hunger beckoning.
Whoever thought this visual spectacle would filter down into every ventricle of shallow fashionista hypocrisy, of what a woman should appear to be...

A parade of skinny mini mannequin skeletons, walking on spikes and thinking 'thin.'
This seems to be the pretence of the reality we're living in.
But since when did 'liberty' mean keeping the temple of body
a prisoner for the delight of an industry?

We endure far more than you will ever see.
Silently nursing wounds from stilettos sat on a toilet seat,
Blotting spots below spotlight mirrors before meeting you for the evening.
Sucking it in so you don't comment on the fact I'm not as thin as that girl in a magazine, whose so photoshopped but worshipped in idolatry,
No one is as perfect or shiny as they may seem.

Flawlessness as visual perfection, is not the liberty we require as a generation,
We are mothers, protectors and carers of those who decide war is better than a conversation,

We will not sit quietly showing you our ankles unless you provide some consolation,
Equality should be as standard to atoms in just another constellation.

Ladies you are the masters of your own projection,
Liberty weeps for those who suffer for visual imperfection,
Your projection shouldn't be about just who you 'appear' to be,
It's about allowing yourself to shine through, flaws and all, healthily.
Declaring yourself to be a real-woman empowered by your own femininity, not defined by the standards of a money-driven industry,
And simply saying 'fuck it, I'll just be me'.

DAVID OLIVER
ENGLAND, UK

BIO

David Oliver began writing poetry in May 2020 as a way to share some much-needed positive energy. As the world was experiencing the effects of Coronavirus, it was a way to connect with the world through the power of words. Sharing the inner thoughts and perspectives with anyone can be a vulnerable thing to do. Through sharing David's poems, he challenged himself to become more confident and honing in on him speaking his truth as he felt that was an experience that he needed.

Through David pushing his personal boundaries he has been able to learn more about himself and become a stronger person and writer. Poetry is a way to express himself freely and to connect to a broader network of people.

BACKGROUND

David Oliver has had a passion for reading and writing since childhood.

Experiences throughout David's life inspired him to study and practice methods to enhance positivity in people's lives whilst developing an understanding of human emotions and behaviour.

He is a published Poet, Reiki Master, Neuro Linguistic Programming Practitioner, Psychic Medium and Tarot reader.

The combination of David's passion and experiences have enabled him to powerfully convey his emotional ideas in an intricate yet easily relatable manner through his poems.

CONTEXT FOR POEMS

The poems that I have submitted contain themes of recognising that personal and social challenges can be overcome if people are willing to be honest about their motives. Giving an opportunity to care about themselves and others, as well as celebrating the positive qualities of life.

CONNECT

Facebook @DO.Wordsmith
Instagram @david_oliver_wordsmith

Release

Shrouds now removed, no more do they smother and hide what needs to be seen, released from the desperate grip of others that held so tightly to keep us from becoming more.
Like footsteps in snow filled with fresh fall, the imprints become invisible never to be retraced, gone forever to not be known again, the sun sets to move on to distant far-away lands.
Farewell and goodbye to the past gone before, it is time now to welcome in future days yet to dawn, after the darkness fades and the morning breaks, the joy of freedom again shines on all.

Blessed

The weight of a feather, so delicate, is phenomenal when it comes out of nowhere and makes it known that the angels are always there.
A small and beautiful miracle meant for you and you alone to lift up your heart from sadness and give a little hope when all seems lost.

Ceasefire

The day they put down their guns, and exchange kindnesses instead of bullets, when leaders guide with a hand we want to take, and trust can be given without condition.
When the most is made of all that has already been created and not discarded on a heap to just rot away, all food is fed to those who are hungry so that they can be healthy and never starving to death.
When all are respected for being who they are so that they can live however they see fit, free of mockery, oppression, prejudice or fear for the very lives that they lead.
I hope for that day and I hope it is tomorrow for there is no reason why it should not be so, on this one planet there is only one people and the one only aim that should be strived for is living of life.

Mindfulness

Embrace and indulge in the *real*, the truths that speak to your soul and help you heal, the vibrations that resonate with love and light, the motions that you can truly feel.
Behold the wisdom that it brings, the great strength of pure truths to lift up your wings, the emotions that enable all that is right, the chorus that our soul gladly sings.

Rewards Well Deserved

Stepping to the fore, as bold as brass and gleaming bright, shamelessly proud of what has been achieved, with no doubt to tarnish the victory celebration.
The journey has been long but the outcome is most certainly worthwhile, the effort has brought us to a place of well deserved power.
This is undoubtedly our time and we are most certainly in the very place where we belong, so long may we enjoy the sweet fruits of our labour so very much deserved.

Fall To Arise

Rain falling down, tears falling harder, feeling so cold and lonely, soaked to the bone.
Your heart heavy and hurting, feeling ready to submit and give up, questioning why you should care.
Then within the ripples and rivulets the image becomes so clear, every angle and aspect reflected to be seen.
Years within seconds of all that has come before, everything lived through to be remembered and embraced, all rush to the present, this single moment in time, reminders of why sometimes we must become uncomfortable to be inspired to become better.

Persistence

These moments need not be enshrouded in painful woes, too heavy to bear and exhausting to endure, emasculating to the point of inability to move on to the next.
There still remains many chances to gain success and victory in the face of adversity, strength remains be in faith that good fortune remains to be found.
Stay the course with trust that it is worthwhile for even though it may not be a clear view ahead, clarity shall soon come to reveal a glorious vision anew.

Elemental

Sometimes we are the mighty mountain, standing strong and steady reaching up high to touch the sky above, sometimes we are the still lake, wide and deep and placidly reflective yet withholding of mysteries within so alluring to the curious.

Sometimes we are the shining sun, bold and bright with burning energy to give life and vitality to all within our constant unerring touch, sometimes we are the silvery moon, changing what we let others see from a thin sliver to a full unabashed display of unique enchanting beauty.

Sometimes we are the supportive Earth, giving to all that rely upon our being to thrive and flourish with good fortune, sometimes we are the tumultuous storm, bringing torrential rain with howling gales to push all that stands in our way as wild power shocks with ferocious light and thunderous roars.

Sometimes we are all of these things and more, from the moment made precious in its brief but amazing manifestation to the captivating vastness of eternal being, constructed of a countless array of varying elements each as different as the other yet similar in their undoubtedly phenomenal existence.

NATHANIEL NEW-CASTLE
(N.N. CASTLE)
AUSTRALIA

BIO

Born in Queensland (QLD) Australia, travelled to Victoria, South Australia, Northern Territory before coming back to QLD to settle and raise a family.

I've worked in retail for 8 years as a computer technician and IT support. Completed a Diploma in Science with the intention of becoming a physicist; a far-reaching goal but the first step in really recognizing what sort of potential lurked within myself. As I have searched to develop and learn about myself professionally, this attribute also flows into my writing and poetry. Always searching for a deeper understanding of myself and how to express this to the world.

Happily married with a small daughter and fur ball of a cat.

I spend my down time enjoying video games, movies, reading, writing, and being dad. Favourite video game: Bloodborne, movie: Shaun of the Dead (almost Hot Fuzz or Starship Troopers), book(s): Eragon series (though Sherlock is climbing up the more I read on), TV Show: IT Crowd, piece of my own work: The Suffering, child: My daughter (though cat comes second).

BACKGROUND

Writing has always been my companion something which I consistently enjoy, a creative medium for me to connect to all facets of myself. From early childhood to now, writing stories was always fun.

Through the journey of life, I questioned within myself if I was a serious writer, a journey many writers go on. Concluding that I am a serious writer who can make a name for myself even on an unrecognised path of life. Poetry itself came from dark times; I started writing raps for fun before they evolved into poems for expression; a psychological medicine. As I breached back into a healthier mindset, my writing faded away. Until now. Now I've recognised writing for what it is and always has been, my calling.

Sure, I dabbled in drawing and animating, programming and film making among other things. But nothing quite captures what I want captured like a good number of words on a blank page. My goal with writing is to firstly publish a collection of all my poetry (or more so what's relevant to the overall theme that captures almost all of my work), then move onto finishing a few short stories I started a while ago and potentially compiling those.

I have some bigger novel ideas I started teasing that I'd like to complete. The eventual end goal is to put my story telling and writing abilities to create a story driven video game. Then? Who knows. Probably more writing.

CONTEXT FOR POEMS

The collection of poems I've written is called 'Scope'. It's me capturing the most prominent things in my scope of vision, firstly being zoomed all the way out to the universe, then gradually zooming in, while making some stops on the way (sun, moon, Earth, nature), so that eventually my own self is what fills the scope's view; and thusly what I see is what each poem is about.

Scope goes in this order: Universe, Sun, Moon, Earth, Nature, Human, Perspective.

The poems start less structured and gradually the structure and complexity of the topic increases. Similarly, the smaller things scientists research, the more complicated and weird things get.

CONNECT
Facebook @natescreativespace

Universe
Its emptiness is filled with anything and everything
Even nothing consists of something as nothing is something
The empty set is a set in itself baring nothing
And nothing is something. And something can't be nothing.
      Everything is something
             Nothing doesn't exist
Much like our imagination, the universe is endless
                                Maybe.
More so of riddles than answers; but it can all be answered
           Spread thin and sporadic
      The universe likes to be dramatic
Look up entropy, it's obvious
Look up black holes and star clusters and galaxies.
Look at how profound it all really is
In this giant particle salad

Sun

The Sun and its repeating, perpetual ignitions
With dramatic effects as explosive as its own cyclic explosions,
Along with mass particle ejection for our nutrition,
Are in part what retains its famous recognition.
Never will it devolve to a red giant in my time set
Nor yours or your next or your next's next, next… next.
Neither will it become a white dwarf,
Extinguished,
Until after Andromeda inevitably hits us.
Assuming it stays out of the firing line,
Which it likely will,
In that oncoming miracle.
Scorching storms and tornadoes of fire,
Flares that breach atmospheres higher,
It's chaotic and destructive and I could think of nothing finer
As the result results in a light that gives us life
That could never otherwise be brighter.

Moon

Beyond twilight when all's dark and no sunshine,
An otherwise masked figure takes the Sun's residual glow
To illuminate our otherwise pitch-black midnight sky.
The presence the Sun gives it, passes gracefully slow
And our perception is branded by cycling phases of the night.
For some, it captivates and engages their emotional growth;
Ultimately for all it activates oceans to shift with the tide.
The Moon influences our Earth by coasting while apart,
Even to bask in its luminance can soothe a tired, weary soul;
It's no wonder our closest celestial body inspires symbolism in art,
Or portrayed a sentient entity like a character made whole.
Its Lunar presence presents us a spectacular, pearly heart;
And with it, a different taste of a moonlit life to stroll.
With the Moon keeping watch, dare you be afraid of the dark?

Earth

Rotating along, we're bound and bogged
By centripetal forces; reverberating gravity's silent song.
A lifestyle here on our 'roughly spherical', sapphire planet
Alters and changes and we can live as total polar opposites
Depending directionally on where our nearest opposite pole is.
An environment that leaves you wet and cold wherever you sit
Or another that leaves you engulfed in a tantalising dry heat;
It's dependent on your prescribed location and geography.
Seasons cycle as the Earth circles around the Sun's majesty,
All while you and I experience each revolution differently.
Whether you weather a storm or bask in calm weather calmly
Surprisingly can be affected by your assigned geology.
The Earth provides only what we can take.
When we can't, we outsmart before changing place.
Seek an expansive forest that's luscious with all sorts of colours
Or a grey, concrete jungle where it's only money that matters.
A serene lifestyle can await you with all conflict peacefully answered;
We got it all.
Alternatively, you can seek out our many fine violent establishments.
Opportunities to become wealthy, or lack thereof in poorer conditions.
It is a privilege to call shots; although options still exist in oppression.
We got it all.
Experience things so soft and beautiful. There's also hideous and rough!
Live gloriously in the light or hidden away in the dark.
Be attracted. Be repulsed. What makes you laugh?
Good. Bad. Nothing more.
We got it all.
And through it all that we have
We have at least one another

Within our Earth and all its splendour.
You can find it all.
Life and death are met in equal force,
But only in life can it be explored.
Through the darkest nights
And brightest of days,
The Earth gives it all.

Nature

Not a single thing could better encapsulate a drive so primal,
Than observing any our Earthly creatures thrive; as entitled.
Removing cognition exposes a natural state so emotional,
So honest, so completely and utterly unbiased
Aside from basing its influence from sheer, unwavering survival;
Aside from instinctively aiding nature to blossom and flourish.
I was stunned to learn, to experience
That a life beyond that of survival exists
For our creatures we share as our neighbours.
Playing, exploring; so many other things betwixt.
Living to survive isn't, at all, all that matters.
I was stunned to learn, to experience
That a life can provide beyond its own measure.
Working with synergy to unbind from stagnation,
From a shackled life unfulfilled by Earths splendour,
In another of nature's own spawned creations.
Its influence can be as dramatic as a warning of predators,
Or as small yet impactful as carrying pollen from tree to tree.
Nothing better represents a persistence in presence
Than admiring plants taking up every spot of residence
In every nook and cranny of the Earth we inhabit.
Our local plant life grows with such resilience,
And is so entirely unphased holding no judgment
Toward our worldly daily goings and dramatisations
Yet asserts itself as required for all life to be triumphant.
I was stunned to learn, to experience
The infinite form plant life gives in numbers
To fit between all our even artificial layers.
Or how effortlessly it can overrun
A now dilapidated memory of our existence.
I was stunned to learn, to experience
How everything is so connected,
And tied but not confined,
By plants and their innate ability

To give us oxygen and nutrients.
Its influence can be as dramatic as hindering a tsunami
Or as small yet impactful as giving bees a purpose.

Human
Me, myself, and I;
Mind, body, and soul.
The mind alive and writhing in unknown;
It's unwise and untested until independent.
Selfishly selfless and oh so wickedly reckless;
Trials begin blind, with naught to reference.
Structured destruction remains equidistant
From beginning and end; both are so elusive.
The mind alive and yearning the known.
It could have been anything, any vessel,
A body shimmering shapeless until shaped
By sculptors, neither benign nor estranged.
Some of which, so romantically draped,
Pluck and peel with nothing left fettered.
Paradoxically to ideals, a body is restrained.
In matter alone it doesn't matter; only a vessel.
Everything shapes the flow of our souls
Into each, these fragile leaking canvases.
It pours, and it purrs, and it often ravages;
A consciousness is defined by its limits.
But these limits are just tools; fidgets.
Delicately bridging bridges and bridges
The flow of our soul's shape everything.
Mind, body, and soul;
Me, myself, and I.

Perspective

                              I never noticed that star before…

Great perspective is never granted, only earned.
Great perspective is elusive, but of great worth.
It was far too easy to resist and reject
A great perspective that knew me best.
So, I learned;
The easier the perspective,
The perspective is for worse.
But it could be worse;
I learnt.
                        Arcturus, it goes by Arcturus…

How can you reject what's made.
What's made permanent stays.
Scars in the mind, they prey,
I learned,
On stars portrayed
And splashed away
To fade.
                        Arcturus. It's so bright…

I reject and detest!
Nothing knows me best,
Not like the darkness.
Why fight?
Beasts can be pets.
No light,
Yet
No rest.
I didn't
Learn.
                      But Arcturus sure is burning brightly tonight…

An abrupt epiphany suddenly reveals a truth so honest,
One that dissolves, the moment it acknowledges,
Anything that questions it as anything other than perfect.
A great perspective could make me a detective,
Forensically piecing the narrative as it should best fit.
I could learn.
So, I learned
The Gloom promises nothing frightening,
Not when I'm familiar now with what lurks within.
Lucidity promises nothing welcoming,
Not when even in daylight can crimes be so grim.
I learned
Everything can be found everywhere.
What you see is what you think, nothing is bare.
It's all just a matter of perspective;
Arcturus burns brightly every night.

LUCY NOVARO
MEXICO

BIO

Lucy Novaro has been writer and editor in different publications in Spanish and some in English. She is former editor-in-chief of Vogue Latin America. She also wrote and edited in other printed editions of Reforma Newspaper in features section; also, has contributed to Glamour in Spanish Magazine.

Her last participation as editor in chief in print was in Eve Magazine in Spanish. She started to do freelancing in blogs in English such as Travel Fashion Girl and started her own blog in 2021 -Beu Magazine-. Lucy has always loved poetry and she has some of her own (unpublished). She also has a podcast in Spotify where she does interviews of artists.

DESTERRADO

A mi padre

Como una fiera al borde del ocaso
La cordura de la vida no te pertenecía
siempre estabas un paso adelante a veces incomprendido.
Ahora perteneces a las más altos vuelos de la vida etérea

Enfrentaste al mundo con valentía y sabiduría
siempre con estilo
Eso, tú me lo enseñaste
Dejaste un legado
Eres libre como un águila en pleno vuelo.
El mundo te quedaba pequeño y decidiste volar.

EXHILED (English)
*A mi padre

A fierce at decline.
The sanity of life was never in your veins
You were always one step ahead, sometimes misunderstood
Now, You belong to the highest realms.

You dealt with life with dignity and wisdom
...That; you taught me
You left a legacy
Be free, like the flying eagle you are
The world was not enough...
...and you decided to fly.

Amazing doors

Detrás de esa puerta…
…hay tantas historias
Un amor a la vida
O un ser que perdimos
Color, Vida, Muerte
Música, reuniones
Amores, romances y pasiones
…tantas historias, tantas…
Como la vida, como la muerte.

Amazing doors (English)

Behind that door…
…there are so many stories
A love for life
Or the loss of a loved one
Color, Life, Death
Music, gatherings
Love, romance and passion
…so many stories so many…
As in life, as in death.

A.J. HAIGH
AUSTRALIA

BIO

A.J. Haigh was born in Australia and grew up in Brisbane throughout her childhood and teenage years. She is a poet that often writes engaging poems about her life experiences which include challenges around mental health, family life and navigating friendships as a teenager. A.J. Haigh has faced some mental health and physical health challenges and through those challenges, she found writing poetry helped her understand those difficulties.

CONNECT

Instagram @theheartfelt.poetry

racing heart
sweaty palms
lack of sleep
drained mind

always hiding how I genuinely feel
always thinking I am burdening people
always feeling a sense of overwhelming
always overthinking things that average people would say I'm crazy for overthinking
always feeling like my world is crushing into my enormous thoughts

— my world

Sometimes i wonder why hurt exists
Sometimes i wonder why someone would emotionally hurt another person
Sometimes i wonder how much hurt you can handle as a person

Hurt isn't just a thing
Hurt isn't just an emotion
Hurt isn't just a feeling
Hurt is a journey you go through
Hurt is something you have to learn to live with

— hurtful journey

That feeling I didn't know what it meant
That feeling I didn't know how it felt
That feeling I always imagined in books
That feeling that took over my anxiety

Until…
My closest friend glowed of that thing I was missing
My life started being surrounded by it
My world became that thing I had missed from my childhood

— E.R.

You chose her
Not over your partner
Not over a stranger
Not over a friend
But over your daughter

I may not understand it
But that is life
Life is a world of choices
Even if they sting your heart

— life is what you make it

NIAMH FRIEL
SCOTLAND, UK

BIO

Niamh is poetry and fiction writer originally from Scotland. She completed her degree at the Glasgow School of Art in Sound for the Moving Image in 2023 and decided to pursue a career as a freelance writer.

Niamh considers herself as someone who can transition from one style to another very effortlessly within writing and styles, this also carries over to her personal life where "Jack of all trades" can describe her. Niamh finds passion within her writing, asking the reader to join her on her journey through words that she shares with you.

INTRODUCTION

Born and raised in a small house tucked away in the woods of

Scotland, Niamh found herself inspired by nature and all things fairytale. A love of writing caused her to pick up the pen at early age, developing a particular interest in short fiction. Inspired by high school poetry workshops from the likes of Miko Berry and Layla Josephine, Niamh began writing regularly and performed two of her works "Mirror Image" and "100 Years" at high school events.

CONTEXT FOR POEMS
The themes of my poems vary but all come from deeply personal experiences; love, heartbreak, self-image. I hope that these poems provide even a slither of the catharsis for you, the reader, as they did for me when writing them.

CONNECT
TikTok @small_t0wn_glasgow
Instagram @smxll_t0wn_witch
niamhfriel27@gmail.com

You

The unfounded expression buried
beneath my simple words
Carries little weight
On your soul.
Rather,
Weighing heavy on mine.

Trying to escape
They arrest my breath.
Held prisoner
Behind my teeth
Lighting fires in my throat
As I attempt to confess

My innocence to you
Is lost in the breeze
The winds of change
Blown away with them all meaning.
Of who I am, was
To you.

Close Enough

Eventually I realised
you were just like the rest of them.
Never truly wanting me,
Keeping me at arms length but always within arms reach.

I was convenient.
Vulnerable, like a sparrow with a broken wing.
I was yours
At least in the space between your thoughts.

Your affections for me dangling on a string,
I would crawl on bruised knees to taste.
A familiar bitterness of what I recognised as love lingered on my tongue.

Your eyes closed as you thought of her,
Holding me tightly to fill the void.
Close enough to her shape, I slotted in beside you,
"Close enough" you thought.

You Cannot Love Me

You cannot love me,
I will not let you.
The pain of heartbreak
Is not worth me cutting open my chest
To let you inside.
You will only set me on fire
And leave me to burn
And then complain that you smell like smoke.

Taking Up Space

Rivers do not carry with them the weight of the rocks beneath,
Fire does not feel the pain of burning flesh.
Air moves freely, without the burden of taking up space.
Earth does not apologise for changing with the seasons.

So why do you shrink yourself to nothing?
Your bones are made of stardust, magic runs through your blood.
Hiding in the shadows will only dampen your cosmic light.

100 Years

The words that roll off our tongues have built nations,
And our actions that take us to great destinations.
We have inspired civilisations,
A new generation of women.

Hips that carry life,
Are gateways to opportunity
With the power to shield from the world,
We provide unity.

For years we were silenced,
Fought to gain unity.
And during World War I,
We went on hiatus
Not to give up, backdown or accept
But to fight for a cause
We shall never forget

But 100 years ago,
We got a voice, a choice, a right to vote
Since then, we've had women in power all across the globe.
Empowering other women to do as they must.
To take a stand, take a chance and to not give up

You see being a woman isn't just a gender
It's a way of life
Through all the pain, suffering and strife
We carry mountains on our backs And life in our arms.
Say words that leave a mark and cry tears that put the seas to shame… no wonder it's our trademark.

You see, we are not just women.

We are pillars of strength that rise up
Through the darkest depths holding our own, it's what we do best.

Mirror Image

Looking at myself, sometimes I ought to cringe.
At how simple, how basic, how utterly pathetic.
Nothing could amount to make this face better.
No amount of money could pay this body's debt to society,
For it is haggard, it is scarred and most of all it is mine.

So I shall sit here, in front of a mirror.
So I shall sit here, trying not to quiver.
So I shall sit here, crying at what I mirror.
The ugly and torn and tattooed freak.

You see, when I was four I looked so innocent.
Now sixteen I look similar to the convicted.
The tattoos that adorn my body have earned me maliciousness.
And the piercings on my face have deemed me un-kissable.

So I shall sit here, hidden behind a wall.
So I shall sit here, trying not to scream.
So I shall sit here, painting myself in your dreams.
The perfect and pretty and docile queen.

For my head is a constant war zone
Constantly torn between fitting in and standing out
But perhaps my only crime, is feeling as though I must stand in line.
Behind a million other "originals".

For that is what you want me to do,
That is how you want me to feel.
So I adorn myself with metal and ink.
Because my satisfaction comes from filling in MY missing link.

So I shall sit here, proud and accepting.
So I shall sit here, knowing I am worthy.

So I shall sit here, with my alternative body that you frown upon.
Knowing that I will still love myself after dawn.

The Lies You Told

There is little left to say,
Words no longer hanging
My body no longer starving
Your scent fading to nothing

I stitch myself together
With hands that have forgotten your touch.
Your voice no longer fills the silence.
My heart does not crave the chaos.

All traces of you
Lost to the sun
All traces of you
Except one

Etched into my skin
Unable to loosen the hold
Breaking under the weight
Of the Lies You Told.

JACQUELINE LEWIS
(FREE)
ENGLAND, UK

INTRODUCTION

I'd like to introduce my Mum, Jaqueline Lewis, who came to Australia from England as a young teenager. My Mum was a true representation of the peace movement in the 60's and 70's in every way. A down to earth free spirit, she was a loving, caring, generous, kind, amazing and had a beautiful soul. A talented poetic artist. A much loved and devoted Mother to 6 children. Writing poetry was a part of Mum's life since she was a child. She learnt to master the art of storytelling and word-smithing and I have fond memories of my Mum writing and telling us stories throughout my life with her.

She had a way about her, no matter where she went, she was always expressing kindness and generosity, always a friend to everyone. She never judged people and lived her life to the fullest and most truthful. Through her words you will see a soul so gentle and free. Poetry was a living breathing embodied experience for my Mum and she has hundreds if not thousands of poems penned to her name.

These are but a slither of her poetry that form part of her prolific collection which was fortunately saved after her passing. You will experience my Mum's unwavering faith in humanity to be real and authentic. You will feel her kind, humble and powerful spirit. Her writing will sweep you away to otherworldly places and just for those moments you can be free just as she would want you to be. Just as she signed off on all her poems 'free'

It was my Mum's dream to see her poetry published and I am proud to honor her name to fulfill one of her dreams. Mum's poetry is as diverse as there are people and her words can make you laugh, or they can make you cry.

- One of Jacqueline's six children

The Bush

What is it about this place,
That makes me want to stay?
I'm in the Australian Highlands,
The bush as some may say.
Faced with drought, flood and fire,
What am I doing here?
Yet as I look around me,
My heart leaps with cheer…
I wake every morning
My bedroom once a shed,
I look out on the river and trees,
I know why, the city I fled!
I take breakfast in my kitchen,
Which nestles at the base of a hill,
Nature abounds and thrills me,
I watch a kookaburra sharpen his bill
As I do my tapestry,
Surrounded by old Ghost Gums,
I try to catch the splendor,
It's all part of the fun.
The beauty and the danger,
Are a way of life each day,
The peace that I find here,
Is the reason I stay.

'Free'

Energy Flow

Only allow into your life
What you are comfortable with.
Only give from your life
What you happily give.
You are your master
Over the mystery of your life
You are free
To choose where to be
Whether happy or in strife
Take time to set in order
Allow your energies to flow
You will surely grow.

'Free'

Guidance

This whole word is in a spin,
Only with love can we win,
Put on your cloak
And your shield,
To this corrupt establishment,
Do not yield.
Discipline your family,
Love them and guide,
Show them our world
Is still alive.
Teach them to care for this earth
And its trees,
Teach them that life
Can be lived with ease.
Hard working we always
Reap what we sow
Show them the peace
We know can grow,
By doing unto others
As you would have them do to you,
This way of life
Will show them what's true.

'Free'

Illusions

Climbing a stairway to dream in phases,
Amongst the stars and heavenly spaces.
Amongst the galaxies I find my way
Hoping to find a place to stay
We go through now
A dreamers reality of illusion,
Hoping not to create confusion.
I'm sitting on the night sand,
The surf is rolling in,
I look up at the moon and stars
To see what they may bring
I lay back now so more heaven I may see,
As I do this I realise
I'm setting myself free.
I engulf upon a mystical cloud,
To see where I may go
Reds, blues, purples and greens,
Flashing lights are what I'm shown.

Now I hear a restless voice
Telling me to come on through,
A big black hole.
It wasn't there before
I'm sure that it just grew.
I take my curiosity and through the hole I go,
Mysteriously I find that time,
Is moving very slow.
Then I see them
'Is it one or four?'
Reaching out to open a star studded door,
I go inside we sit and stare
No speech is needed,
They know why I'm there.

A restless voice speaks out again,
Asking this human if it's adventure or game?
I speak out and ask what he means?
'Life' he said 'is full of dreams'
'Dreams' I said, 'will you grant me one'?
'Of course' he said 'your from the land of the sun'

All of the sudden there are thousands of clouds,
Each one full of innumerous crowds,
People more people for as far as I see,
All of them laughing
In their clouds they are free.

Then I see a small red car
Its filling the sky it's quite bizarre:
I climb on in it's a Mercedes Benz,
I'll stay on this trip until it ends,
Buzzing around on planet and star,
Can't really tell if I'm near or far,
I park on a planet - it's STUNNING!
That's when I see a meteorite coming,
We're hit - I awaken,
Where's my car?
That's when I see a small red star,
Zapping out past the milky way,
Here in reality my dream can't stay.
I sit up now on wet night sand,
Wondering if I'll ever understand,
Transgression between the reality and illusion
But I know that Mercedes
Is worth the illusion.

'Free'

Invisible Walls

Life is what you make it
Or so they say,
As long as all the rules,
You're willing to obey.
Corruption, pollution leading the way,
Greeds and wants
Causing scaly decay.
Money is the center
Of all that they do,
Ruling out many things
That really is true.
Making it impossible
For people to live,
War hunger and fear,
Are the things they give.
All tied up, you can't get away,
Their prison surrounds us
Open display!
Eyes are now open
That won't look away,
Our planet needs more love today!
Freedom comes from sharing and caring
Not by investing in all the despairing,
Look after our species
Look and see,
We all have the right
To be free.

'Free'

Unsure

I want to be treated with love and respect,
I want to feel that I'm not dead yet,
I want my family to be proud of me,
I want to be happy, loved and free.
I don't think I'm as bad as they think,
Being avoided is pushing me to the brink.
I feel like a contagious disease,
They don't realise how much my heart bleeds,
I know I've screwed up,
Many time in my life,
Always I pull myself out of strife.
All I've ever wanted was love and respect,
Though I have learnt this not to expect.
Expect it I don't but it hurts deep inside,
When I see from my life,
They'd rather hide.
Rarely a letter,
A phone call at its best
Is kept very short
I cause tension at the nest.
I realise they all have a life of their own,
I'm part of a family
Yet - I'm so alone.

I'm proud of myself
I'm doing quite well,
There's negative factors,
On these I don't dwell.
There are so many things,
I want to achieve,
In all my beliefs I still believe,
I know in many ways
We all disagree

I also know one day
They will see,
I can make it on my own,
For my life is my castle,
In which I've grown.
I've grown to learn
I'm really quite strong,
I also know my road is long,
I know I can cross
Any obstacle in my way,
In my life my pride has the final say,
My pride says keep going your doing alright,
Don't with the family get so uptight,
When I achieve what I'm heading for,
I know they'll be proud of me, for sure.

'Free'

Humanness

What is happiness? I'm trying to see
Who am I? What's inside of me?
Lost, confused, full of doubt
Keep on knocking, but can't get out
Is happiness being on my own?
Living my life, until I'm fully grown
What do I mean by fully grown?
I don't understand, I have never known
I know I keep searching
What am I looking for?
I thought it was love
But there is always a flaw
Is it the feeling that floods through my veins
When I look at nature after it rains?
Is it sitting by the river under a shaded tree
Soaking in thoughts, writing quite free?
Is it dancing to a beat that strikes in my heart?
Music I feel plays a very big part
Is it emotions you feel when embraced
By little children whom in your life have been placed?
Is it down by the beach having a swim?
Laying on the sand, satisfying a whim
Is it caring about people and showing you care?
Even their problems, your willing to share
Is it knowing god our fathers love
Pouring out peace from heaven above?
I guess all these things, I really do believe
So why in my heart, do I still grieve?
Why do I feel like I am ready to fail…..

'Free'

SHERR MARIE ALTAMIRANO DIAZ
(BULLET)
CANADA

BIO

Sherr Marie Altamirano Diaz originally from the Philippines and migrated with her family to Toronto, Ontario, Canada in 1992. She graduated from York University with bachelor's degree in nursing with Special Honours. She is currently working at Walmart Canada as a Department Manager of OMNI. Sherr has been writing poetry since the age of 14. When she is not working, Sherr Marie finds joy in baking, reading, playing the piano and singing. She also collaborates song writing either with her aunt or her cousin when time permits. Sherr believes that if the readers can relate and feel every word of her poems that she has done her job as a poet.

INTRODUCTION

My name is Sherr Marie Altamirano Diaz. I write poems, songs and essays. Poetry for me is a door to one's mind and soul. It can clearly express one's emotions when it is hard to open up to someone without being judged. I love poetry because I find solace in writing it as well as reading it. I started writing poetry at the age of 14 but intermittently. Unfortunately, I have lost all the poems I had written back then. By 2020, I have been more actively writing poetry.

CONNECT
Facebook @sherrmarie.diaz
Instagram @sherrapples
www.lineofpoetry.com/bullet

"Time"

It's time to take what belongs to me
Give myself all the loving and attention
All the giving has made me exhausted
Mentally and physically drained
Losing track of all the priorities
Although no regrets in what was given
But drifting away to who and what I can be
A road that shouldn't be less travelled
What is done though cannot be undone
Sulking about the past is just unnecessary
Time to fight back and take a stand
To bring back a better version of me
To see the strong woman once again
The one full of life and positivity
Time to rise above the water
And like a Phoenix rising from its ashes
Conquering life's goals and dreams
And start the fire deep within
To be among the stars that light up the sky.

"Twilight Zone"

I am standing in the midst
Surrounded by a thick mist
As if I'm floating in space
Shadows prowling.
Cannot make out as to what it is
Or who could it be
But I feel like someone is watching
I can feel their stare piercing through me
The silence is overwhelming
But silent screams and cries are echoing
Vibrating inside of me
I can feel it in every bone of my body
Scary thoughts going through my head
Is it just my mere imagination
Or something deep within
Trying to ripped out the beast in me
And pulling into the darkness.

"Mask"

A thousand smiles
But inside she's ripping apart
Feeling raw deep within
Having been through a lot
Withstanding all the pain and heartaches
Putting the mask to deceive everyone
Of all the struggles she's going through
The silence is deafening
Wanting to explode
Yet she has to hold it in
Composure is always expected of her
Her dream in life is simple
No amount of money can buy
But life just wanted to test her more
To see how strong she can be.
Tiredness is visible
But in so much denial
Silently crying inside
Feeling all alone in this world
If only loneliness could kill
She died a hundred times
She's not asking to be saved
But for someone to be there for her
Even just once...

"Space"

The space that you and I used to belong
A moment in time of love, memories and pain
As if nothing can break it
In the blink of an eye...
Everything collapsed
No explanation as to why.
Until now, it is still the unspoken moment
Never thought that it will haunt me
Every time I go to our space
Tears filled my eyes
My heart feels so broken
Knowing time cannot bring you back
All what's left is the love you've given me
Our short time together on this earth
As I listen to your favourite song
The memories linger on...
I know you and I will meet again
But in a different time and space.

"My Reflection of Life"

She stared at her reflection
At the mirror in front of her
She saw the little girl
The one who's shielded from everything
Full of life and laughter
Not a care in the world.

Her youthful self appeared
Threading the waters
Strong-headed and fierce
Trying to conquer the world
Full of dreams and ambitions

The breeze went through the window
Reality sets in...
As the image staring back at her
The fine lines on her face
The puffiness of her eyes

She realized how much she'd aged
She often wonders...
Where did time go
As reflection shows
The battle scars written all over her face.

"My Very Special Love"

Your love is my lighthouse
That guides my way into your heart
And brings brighter days

You are one special love
So blessed to have
A divine gift from heaven above.

You are my home
The completeness of my being
The life of my heart and soul.

The depths of my love for you
Is beyond the deepest oceans
Immeasurable and pure.

I will always love you
No matter what you go through
For my heart knows only YOU.

"You"

In my heart
I hope you stay
No matter how stubborn I can be

In my life
I would like you to be
Building a home with me

In my soul
You will see
The purity of my love for you.

In God, I've asked for you
To guide my way to you
To unite us for a lifetime.

I know nothing's perfect
But I will take my chance on you
For I found my happiness in loving you

"Chaos"

In a world full of chaos
How can one see hope
The endless fighting
Greediness and power hunger
Pointing of fingers amongst themselves
Not one admitting who instigated it
Everyone trying to prove something
Everyone seems to be always right
Money, power and greed are the ideologies
Causing torment and destruction
Playing like God with everyone's lives
Amidst this troublesome world
Innocent children are being ignored
Mass murder circling the block
Just to prove their point
Brokenness seen on the battlefield
Rubble and lifeless bodies scattered around
Justice has come and gone
This is the death of the society
The extinction of humanity.
Created by our very own selfishness.

"Scattered Pieces"

How do you pick up
And put back together
The scattered pieces of yourself
When hope and strength are gone

How can you see the sunshine
When all there is just darkness
The faith you have in yourself
Seems have left you behind

The joy that used to be in your heart
Have dissipated like ashes
Floating endless in the air
Travelling with no destination.

The horizon seems blur at the moment
Heavily burdened of the circumstances
Drowning in misery in this so-called life
In spite of it all, hope springs eternal
That there's light at the end of the tunnel.

"Losing Myself"

Dark clouds hovering over me
Like a storm about to come around
Feeling lost and with uncertainty
In the journey I'm embarking on
I feel stuck on this road
Riding the wave of the raging sea
With no direction in sight
The hope that used to light up the spark
Has temporarily left me hanging on a cliff
Feeling alone and depressed
As if everything has crumbled inside
The perspective on life seems adrift
The jest for life has ceased to exist
With no chance of gaining back
Who I used to be..
How will I?
How can I?
When I don't have the strength
To even stay afloat...
And bring back the stronger side of me.

TK CASSIDY
UNITED STATES OF AMERICA

BIO

TK Cassidy started writing at the age of seven. Her first novel took twenty-four years to write while life led her through thirty-eight of the fifty United States and placed her in Australia and Guam for a time.

TK has a Bachelors in English & Library Science, a master's in library science and a Doctorate in Virtual Education. She worked as a children's librarian for twenty-five years.

While in Guam, TK authored over one-hundred-and-fifty children's stories as a columnist for a local magazine, for which she was the recipient of Guam's Maga Lahi award (named for the ancient Chieftain of the Chamorro). Her best-known story, Dolphin, Dolphin ushered her into becoming a travelling storyteller nicknamed 'Dolphin Lady', traversing Guam and the surrounding islands before returning to the United States. Since retirement, she's turned out one novel per year, edits for several authors and is an active member of the Tuscaloosa Writers and Illustrators Guild.

CONNECT
Facebook @tk.fleming
www.tkcassidywrites.com

Free range toes
(Inspired by Dr. Rosemarie Caillier, podiatrist par excellence)

There will come a day in the not-too-distant future
that I won't be able to do all the things I'm used ta.

When that time comes, I'll gladly accept your aid.
All the while remembering how little that you get paid.

I'll be meek and I'll be kind as we dress me for the day.
I'll be glad to agree with almost anything you might say.

I'll eat the food you make with kind words and a smile.
I'll even let you help me bathe, trying not to make it a trial.

I'll forego my love for my brightly coloured nails
As we sit and chat quietly about all the day's details.

Only one thing will cause a problem and this I can't deny.
I'll argue about shoes every time and here are the reasons why.

Unless you want to arise the beast in me and start a war you'll lose,
For the love of all things living, do NOT enclose my feet in shoes.

I hate the feel of the damp leather rising up a blister, causing
all that hurtin'.
Of all the things I dislike in the world, wearing shoes is the
most certain.

I'll fight you and kick and bite and maybe even squeal
If you try to force that hard leather around my tender heel.

And Lord protect your families, all your kith and kin,
If you ever try to put flip flops in between my toe skin.

I'll teach you how to 'toe' my feet in bulky warm wool socks
How to roll the cuffs down just so far until the fabric locks.

I'll wear my 49ers slippers happily or a pair of slide-ons if you think it best
But I can't abide the feel of sweaty, stinky feet and there I do not jest!

I love the feel of my free-range toes on tile, carpet or wood.
That lovely, unbound feeling just as Nature intended, they should.

So, remember when I'm old and grey and ready to take a doze,
I lived a fabulous life – rarely strapping down my free-range toes.

A View of Poetry

They say that boxing is art –
A sweet science they call it.
But I do not understand how hurting
One another can be considered legit.
Ghouls cheering for pain and blood
Are likely to send me into a fit.

The "art" of war is another that
Most causes my upheaval.
Killing and maiming other people
Can't be anything but less than evil.
Knowing this goes on each day makes
My soul skitter off like a tiny weevil.

I also don't understand poetry.
Please help me with this poor view.
When so much can be explained
And brought to life anew …
With all the glorious, brilliant words,
Why be limited to just a few?

Nor do I understand the works of
Jackson Pollock, Franz Kline and crew.
When you can recreate a perfect copy
Of a dog, person and even a drop of dew,
why will someone pay so much money
For paint on a canvas thrown askew.

I'm afraid my feeble mind, which is
By many considered agile and oddly inventive,
Will never grasp the concept of an
Obscured word or blob of paint suggestive.

I don't want to work so hard to figure out
what each author and every painter meant.
With their hidden meanings, clandestine shapes,
mysterious clouded images and trees oddly bent.

I want to look at pretty pictures that I can recognize
And read stories full of meaning spread out before my eyes.
So … help me, artist and poet, to expand my feeble mind
To understand and enjoy what you do, you wild, crazy guys.

YANE KRITSKI DE OLIVEIRA

BRAZIL

BIO

Apart from writing poetry, Yane has had a very interesting life. They have been scuba diving since 2004. Certified as Scuba Dive Instructor in 2007. Which took them to many work trips around Brazil coast line and paradisiac islands. They taught Science to Elementary and Primary School, Biology to High School Students, English to kids, teens and adults.

Yane wanted to come to Australia since they were 13 years old, but was only possible in their 30s.

They started out as a waiter/waitress and as a cleaner. After two months Yane fell in love with their current fiancée. After meeting each other, building a deep and unbreakable bond Yane went to South Australia to work in an Aboriginal

Community where their fiancée was a remote nurse.

Yane has worked as an assistant teacher at schools until covid hit it, and the school closed. After that they have moved to aged care. Where they have acquired much more experience and knowledge about the community.

They moved with their partner to Brisbane where they started to work as a Support Worker with people with disabilities for over the past three years. In January 2024 they went back to the Remote Aboriginal community, where Yane works as a NDIA - Community Connector. Supporting Aboriginal people with Disabilities in South Australia.

BACKGROUND

Yane is born and raised in South America.

Brazil is my home where they were brought up and have a deep connection to. The city which they were birthed in was mainly cloudy and always rainy, AKA the city that has the whole seasons in one day. Curitiba.

Life was experienced like a mocktail of hardship, trauma and abuse, garnished with lunacy. Through a world of lunacy a connection with writing begins like a amber around a campfire. Now fully fledged poet and author, Yane is a force to be reckoned with their vibrant world view and authentic poetry connecting to the reader immediately. Creating an emotive journey of their view of the world.

First, they wrote about their feelings, their anguishes, and their fears and guilt. Then, they started to write about other people, lives, description, painting in letters, their resemblance.

Finally, to channel, with the person they were writing about, they started to ask 6 words, about their life, what matters, what define them, or even first words that pop up to their thoughts for no reason. Which Yane uses as their brand, poetry with six words in six minutes.

CONTEXT FOR POEMS

Yane draws the reader in by expressing deep emotions through their words, the poems you are about to read cross over multiple countries and seas. Taking you on a journey through my childhood, adolescence and then my adulthood.

With a mixture of styles from poetry with six words in six minutes to a progression of different styles of writing poetry. The reader gets to enjoy the journey of a poet's life writing.

Their favorite poem is "My home is the sea." Yane wrote specially to people that have never encounter the ocean, the sea, the coast, before. They wanted to describe as much as they could for the reader to have the taste of the ocean itself. The poem Little Playground reminds them their childhood and it was very painful to write. While Definition poem is about their process to start loving someone, and how is scary to let it go. Let this feeling flows into you.

CONNECT
Instagram @my_soulpoems

Parquinho (Portuguese)
Curitiba, July 19th, 2015

Quer algo mais depressivo
Que barulho de balanço?
Me lembra minha infância
Quando ficava sozinha
No parquinho

Ia vinha ia vinha

E quando queria
Me animar
Balancava tão alto
E quando estava
No ápice
Pulava
Para o salto
Da felicidade

Ou da morte
De um braço
Ou perna
Quebrada
Uma mistura
De medo e anseio
De angústia e receio

E no meio
As vezes
pensava direito
E desistia
Fazendo com que
O balanço se torcesse inteiro
De volta a realidade

Chega de barulho

Sigo meu rumo

Little Playground (English)

Is there something more depressing
That a swinging noise?
Reminds me of my childhood
When I was alone
On the playground

Coming and going
Coming and going

And when I wanted
To be cheered up
I swung so high
And when I was
At the peak
Jump
For the happiness
Leap

Or face death
One arm
Or leg
Broken
A mix
Of fear and longing
Of anguish and fear

And in the middle
Sometimes
I used to think straight
And would give up
Causing a complete twist
On the swing
Back to reality

No more noise

I follow my course

Definição (Portuguese)
Curitiba, February 25th, 2017

Procurei poemas que definissem
O que sinto
Mas nenhum se encaixa
Se enquadra
Resolvi escrever
Me envolver ainda mais
Com você
Agora me vejo
Em um momento
No meio
De um oceano
Plano
Me encanto
Me espanto
Com esse anseio
Ao mesmo tempo
Intenso
Sereno
Como um sopro do vento
Do começo de uma tempestade
Contínuo
Que causa um alarde
Bate em minha porta
Uiva lá fora
Minha decisão
Já foi tomada
Abrirei a porta
Tomarei essa chuva na cara
Esparsa
Mesmo que machuque
Caia algumas pedras
Dispersas

Corra o risco de
Pegar uma gripe
Voltar com a terrível
E maldita
Rinite

Definition (English)

I looked for poems that defined
What I feel
But none of them fit
Aligned it
I decided to write
Get involved even more
With you
Now I see myself
In a moment
Between flat and
The ocean
I am enchanted
I am amazed
With this longing
At the same time
Intense
Serene
Like a breath of the wind
From the beginning of a storm
Continuous
That causes a fuss
Knock on my door
Howl outside
My decision
Has already been taken
I will open the door
I'll take this rain in my face
Scattered
Even if it hurts
Drop some rocks
Diffuse

Take the risk of
Catch the flu
Back with the terrible
And damn
Rhinitis

Minha casa é o mar (Portuguese)
Curitiba, January 9th, 2015

Toco meus pés na areia
Caminho em direção ao mar
Meus calcanhares
Afundam
Na areia fofa
E quando eu os levanto
Causam um barulho único
Que lembra um grilo
Mais agudo
Sinto a brisa
O sal no ar
Alguns tocam em meus lábios
Trazidos pelo vento
Sei
Estou perto da água salobra
Me arrisco a sentir o frio
Amenizar o sol
O encontro das temperaturas opostas
Arrepia a minha nuca
Caminho
Passo meus dedos sobre a água
E como seda eles transpassam
Através
Mergulho
Abro meus olhos
Tudo nublado
Como se fosse míope
Não consigo ver nada certo
Com linhas retas
Vou retornando a superfície
Estou sem ar
Mas quero ficar

A sensação
Aquela disposição
Então minha mão alcança
A camada
Sinto o sol e solto
Aquele ar filtrado
Respiro o ar puro
Minha boca salga
Olho pra cima
E como mágica
Meu corpo flutua
O sol aquece, ilumina
Meus olhos
Caio um pouco com a testa para trás
Até molhar minhas sobrancelhas
E vejo então
Estrelas do mar

My home is the sea (English)

Touch my feet in the sand
Path towards the sea
My heels
Sink
On the soft sand
And when I lift them up
They cause a unique noise
That resembles a cricket
More acute
I feel the breeze
The salt in the air
Some touch my lips
Blown by the wind
Know
I'm close to brackish water
I risk feeling the cold
Soften the sun
The meeting of opposite temperatures
Chills the back of my neck
Path
I run my fingers over the water
And like silk they pierce
Through
Dive
I open my eyes
All blurred
Like it's short-sighted
I can't see anything right
With straight lines
I'm returning to the surface
I'm out of breath
But I want to stay

The Feeling
That disposition
Then my hand reaches out
The layer
I feel the sun and I'm loose
That filtered air
I breathe in the fresh air
My mouth spices with salt
I look up
And like magic
My body floats
The sun warms, illuminates
My eyes
I fall a little with my forehead back
'Til I wet my eyebrows
And then I see
Starfish

Name: Janice
Words: Joyous - Enjoyable - Joking - Jovial
Brisbane, April 27th, 2023

I think about a day
About a time
Sometime
In the world with out
Us
Still will be joyous?
Or just sorrow?
Maybe not
Maybe no one will remember
But the plants
But the cells
But the carbons
The atoms
Still will be our memory DNA
Recorded for life
So we will be part of the whole
Somehow until the end
Or the beginning of a new age
Enjoyable thinking this way
Made my day
Or it's just me joking about
The eternal life
Being jovial
About that
It's just another
Way of being
Disconnected of this kind of matter
I prefer
To be better

Name: Alex
Words: Profound - Amber - Cuff - Dusk - Shoelace - Calling
Sydney, July 25th, 2018

I'm calling your name
But it's still the same
Emptiness
Loneliness
I feel like
A mosquito
Trapped in an amber
Even the dusk
Make me smile
It's a trial
To tight my shoelace
In peace
Through the surface
I pray
I surrender
I dry my tears with my cuff
And the thoughts go one

Name: Alex
Painting Alex in words

Sydney, July 25th, 2018

Bright eyes
Hidden
Between the yellow light
Nice eyebrows
With lashes
Also, wrinkle's
Deep
Like
His tears
That touch
In his defined
Nose
Oppose
To a whole
Universe
Make
A propose

Name: Unknown
Words: Fear - Freedom - Hysteria - Hoodwink - Love - Outrageous
Sydney, October 7th, 2018

My freedom
Depends on my choice
I fear
To disappear
Sometimes
Mime
It's the only way
I can show what do I think
Hoodwink
Deceive
Continues
Love inside
Outrageous
Become famous
Hysteria
It's my fantasy
To come back
My old time
Should I?

Name: Kate
Words: Ocean - Stars - Love - Happiness - Freedom - Wild

Sydney, November 10th, 2018

In my wild soul
I flow
My love
For the ocean
Transcend
By my skin
My bones
This freedom
That I feel
I see
Through
The stars

Perhaps
Happiness
Is overrated
Our seek
Shouldn't be
Around the bush
Push
Push
Over the shush

KYLA JAY
CANADA

BIO

Kyla Jay is an author and poet from Ontario, Canada. In 2019 she self-published her debut poetry collection titled *A Story* and is currently reworking the anthology into a polished second edition with an expected release date sometime this year. She loves to take poetic inspiration from the world around her as well as her own personal experiences. Kyla tends to write openly about the darker parts of life, including her struggles with mental illness, chronic pain, and childhood trauma. She hopes by sharing her honest experience that it will help end the stigma around these sensitive topics and help others feel less alone.

CONTEXT FOR POEMS

The first 7 poems included in this collaborative anthology

were previously published in Kyla Jay's debut poetry collection *A Story* ©2019 and showcase poems she wrote between 2009-2019. The last 3 poems included in this collaborative anthology are more recent poems written between 2019-2024 and will be featured in her next poetry collection when it is released. Though this is only a small sample of her work, all the poems you see here have been carefully selected to represent Kyla's unique style and voice, and to demonstrate her personal growth as a poet and writer.

CONNECT
Facebook @Kyla-Jay-Author
Instagram @kylajaywriting
TikTok @kylajaywriting
www.amazon.com/author/kylajay
www.kylajay.ca

DIARY

I wrote today
a story of pain
out of my mind
and onto a page
I cried
and the tears
washed it all away

THE TEMPEST

you are my rain
on sunny days
when my heart burns
aches
for the thunder
the storm
the serenity of the calm
after the tempest

FLAWLESS

sadness is my consolation
misery is my solace
desolation is my repose
the dark can be so flawless

ORIGINAL

every word has been said before
every excuse has been used
every path has been walked upon
every emotion abused
someone has felt this
someone has heard
someone has listened
and someone has learned
we are all copies
of a different you
different hair
different smile
same mind
same thoughts of a different kind
bound by limits and laws
conditioned to think in a box

RED

red
the colour of blood
red
the colour of rage
red
dragged through the mud
red
and placed in a cage

CONGRATULATIONS

I have so much to do
but only so much of me
to do a million small things
I have to break myself
into a million small pieces
to achieve
what they can achieve
in one piece
but I stand there
a shattered mess
amongst those who are whole
to celebrate
the same
goal

A STORY

meaningful scribbles
on an empty page
filled with stories
of love and rage

NOSTALGIA

A young girl walked alone along the shore
The moon shone brightly upon her as her bare feet waded through the cold sand
She was not afraid
For the waves were her brothers
And the stars were her sisters
The chill in the air was like a refreshing glass of cold water
She sunk her toes into the frigid shallows
Quietly humming along to the melancholic ballads her mother used to sing
After endless nights and spontaneous road trips to the middle of nowhere
And enough picturesque sunsets to last her a lifetime
She found harmony and balance
In the small joys the world once brought her

RESURRECTION

I breathe in the flames
And let them cleanse my soul
I exhale the darkness
Simmering on the coals

I have been so frigid
And weak
I have been so dispirited
And meek

But now I shall begin anew
Scorch the ache from my heart
And melt away these glacial chains
For a brand-new start

Let the pyre be my fortress
And the smoke be my guard
Choke these demons from my body
Until they are burnt and charred

And as I rise from the ashes
I give praise to the Earth
For without Her fire
I would never find rebirth

IDIOSYNCRATIC

She dances precariously
Like a bull in a china shop
Hesitant to disturb the fragile atmosphere around her
Twirling and gliding cautiously
Across the polished marble floors
Beautifully and tragically
To the beat of her own drum
Humming along to lyrics that she does not know
Her head bowed
Her eyes closed
Her feet moving of their own accord
Enchanted by a melody
As rhythmic and mysterious as she is

RHETORICAL ARTZ
UNITED STATES OF AMERICA

BIO

Rhetorical Artz is a performing poet who loves paradox and dystopian fiction, treats watching an interview like going to the movies, and seeks what's epic every day. From his artistry's birthplace of Pittsburgh PA, he has received recognition of being the 2016 #1 ranked slam poet in the city, premiered on national and international slam stages, and was honoured in the 2020 Pittsburgh anthology "In the Shadow of the Mic" celebrating 3 decades of artists who shaped the cities poetry slam scene.

While acknowledging the accolades, he more readily appreciates people watching words onto paper, then performing them interpersonally with friends (and contemporaries) like Fianna McDonald. Having taken his performance poetry across the U.S. and around the world, his best work comes from conversations with close friends (himself included), walks in nature, and contemplating the nature of the universe.

Over a decade of creative accomplishment, while engaging in life's meaningful moments, has taught him that "the world is a poem that our lives write, our hearts hear, and our souls speak into existence. To be a poet is to converse with the cosmos our world exists in, connect its stars into constellations, and convey them to the world at large. Not everyone is a stargazer, but the awareness of stars above reminds us we are stars ourselves."

CONNECT
Instagram @rhetoricalartz
TikTok @rhetoricalartz

In Your Element

I know how to cry,
cause I've watched the rain
as the water drops down onto the earth.

I see why it may be worth it
letting tears fall down on my own face
and then face the ground like rain clouds
so the world knows what it looks like
to be the salt of the earth.

The phrase basically means people of great kindness, reliability, or honesty.
I've honestly never seen something so true to its way than when rain hits dirt,
showing us that life can get muddy sometimes-
that we can get bloody sometimes-
especially when we're hurt.

In those moments of pain,
I know how to not run away.
because I've seen the earth stay still
despite my attempts to move it forward.

It stands the test of time
so when time tests me
I can withstand it, stand with it, and understand
that to stand under a banner
of belief in why you're here
doesn't mean that you won't fear,
or that as you stand your ground
that the ground you stand on won't shake
cause even the earth at times quakes.

And when it does,
I know that it's okay to take a breath
cause I know the air.

How it allows me to speak so I can reach heights
I might have thought impossible
If I hadn't flown at altitudes where the air gets as thin
as the chances of success are,

but that as long as there is air
that can be inhaled in
and exhaled out
I can shout to the world
that "I will not give up!"

Even if the path to proving the worth of these words is long winded
and there's moments of loneliness and darkness.

Cause I know that it just takes a spark of inspiration
to create light.
I've watched fire ignite before,
witnessed it shine in the sky
and strike onto the floor.

I know that the brightness of who you are,
as a uniquely created human being,
isn't just something you just ignore;
it's something you let shine.

Cause the light
that can illuminate from mankind
isn't all that different from the light your find
showing us the rainbow after the rain goes away,
or when gazing at stars in the darkest of nights
hours before the sun starts to glow again.

How could I possibly witness all this happen ?
Experience it every night and day?
And believe anything other than the fact
that making a living being in your element is okay.

Even if that element has seasons
where it seems scarce,
I know it will be followed by seasons
where it's so abundant
that it encompasses the entire world you live in.

Give in to the element that you so often connect to.
The element that forms the mirror that reflects you.

So you can see yourself,
learn what makes you come alive,
and more importantly
discover your way of remembering…
when you forget,
to live in your element.

Mint

The mint plant survives.
So does she.
It repeatedly dies,
yet forever seems to grow back from its roots.

She's in two minds:
insurance,
supposedly peace of mind,
and insurance claims,
where help's unable to be claimed
while bills backflip in the air towards therapy,
trying to figure out the cost before its descent.

The cost hasn't landed yet.
Neither has the therapy.

She is in two minds:
healing's a never-ending journey
that's not monetary
but money makes it happen
and most of what happens
is physical
not mental
Yet money is a mental construct
thus mental health should be taken as literal fucking wealth
which is as backwards as the backflip of those bills
now being taken up by the winds of
"how the fuck do I appraise something society is not aware enough of to workship?"

She is in two minds:
She hates capitalism
She should;

we all secretly do,
but some of us aren't good at keeping secrets
that weren't meant to be kept.

She starts to hum.
Buttons beep.
Stuff is moved.
Soon there's silence.

The mint plant could thrive,
would take over the whole garden,
if given the chance.

She would too.

Yet that patch of mint land is a church in the wilds.
Is in no sure way insured.
Yet its space is claimed as its own,
with the only peace of mind made apparent
lies in the time she puts in
and the timeline in between.

The in between
of paradoxes repeating,
a perfect place for two perfectly minted minds:
Impermanent.
Eternal.

Random Wait

You squirrels are dope as hell!
These ADHD, teenage angst mother-   fuckers
scurry round randomly then suddenly stop
like they just got trapped in a snapshot.

Squirrels will still themselves.
Humans rarely will.

Sure we don't always talk out loud,
but in our minds, we somehow find
some shit to scurry to like-

when she wrote to me why we are friends
I felt why relationships exist,
saw every single star in the sky
all blink at once-

Once when I was a child,
while on a U.S. family road trip
to see my grandparents
9 states away from my own,
my spirit left my body.
Not metaphorically,
oh no my spirit was serious about this.

It melded into the trees
until I became one
with each and every one,
until I experienced a connection
reflected in everyone.

I have been searching
for that feeling ever since.

Tonight
might be my first clue
since then.

When she told me why we are friends
her words ended a solitary confinement
I thought I was fine with,
'til I smelled the freedom
from one whiff of her words.

When I heard her words
from my voice
I had no choice
but to pause,
to still my squirrely mind
from re-finding its imprisonment.

Reminded me of the dope squirrels
in those trees that became me.
Those ADHD, teenage angst mother fuckers
scurrying round randomly
suddenly stopping
like they just got trapped in a snapshot.

When she told me why we are friends
I saw the bigger picture,
could see each and every united state of minds,
would trace all the stars,
finding our connections
in each and every one,
as everyone
who looked up
all blinked at once-

then,
all at once...
...it's almost gone
and from once
to next
I'm off to some new X
marking another spot
for tasks to be treasured-

"Can I say something?"
"Can you just stand up?"
"Can we just Breathe...deeply?"
"A lot has happened today."
"Take it in...".

Squirrels
be dope as hell,
but that stillness,
she instil   s in me...
is heaven.

Steps Without Land:

Today this 5-dollar coffee
is the price I pay for reflection
in the transient wooden therapy chair
at the coffee shop across the street.

To step off my campus
of higher education
is to unlearn the ghosts
that haunt their halls.
and mine.

For the next hour and a half
I can't receive calls
rarely meant to be answered,
mostly made to be seen
as paths untaken.

Our interconnected world
makes the paths we didn't take
so much louder than the ones we chose
that we barely hear our footsteps along the way.

I am often so plugged in
that I don't see the footsteps made
moving me forward.

Makes me wonder
if I even made them?
if what moves my fingers
across these keys
has anything to do with me?

These thoughts will pass like the 5 dollar coffee,

rivering down my throat to well taught oceans,
and I'll be brought back.

Then I will stand up
from this transient wooden therapy chair,
cause you can only sit
in an uncomfortable seat
for so long.

As I walk away *I'll wonder:*
"What if I stayed just a bit longer?"
"What if I let the spirit of those thoughts
linger like the ghosts do at school?"
"What if I unlearned all the way,
became an utter fool,
a completely useless utility for society?"

Pointless.
Unappraised.
Free....

The Burlesque Manikin

The burlesque manikin is buried underneath a Swedish
luxury neighbourhood,
with it's long flowing silk dress draped down pass the knees,
and a pair of shades between the plastic nose and forehead.

It used to be the first thing seen when stepping into the former
strip club.
Once the only form of income in the poorer part of town,
the club now stands as a relic
of almost religious importance.
Those who remember what once was,
see it and pause, frozen in times when being poor
meant being anonymous, not ostracized

Despite the cost…the strip club was free.
So was the Ole Kings food cart
for anyone exiting this sanctum in the early morning AM.
I am standing where strangers weren't strange,
where strippers and customers linked up after hours.

Not to fuck.
Just to talk.

To laugh at the way Stella clipped her heels
as she walked through the stage curtain.
How Darrs couldn't get a dollar from his pocket after his 4th drink,
and always ended up throwing his whole wallet on stage.

All while the Ole King served his citizens the last of his empanadas
and pop,
always the worst of his batch…
but they were free
and so were we.

Now all I see are luxury houses.
The Ole Kings cart has become the New Prince food truck.
Comes by every Thursday,
charges too much for way too little.

Humans walk out their homes
the same way the strippers stepped onto stage,
still putting on a show.

And I'm still here.

So is everyone else from the old days.
They just don't got bodies no more,
so they embody those who are here,
imitations of what once was,
buried by plastic surgery,
stripped down into an idea of something real,
a burlesque manikin
buried underneath a Swedish luxury neighbourhood,
with its long flowing silk dress stopping before the knees,
and a pair of shades between the plastic nose and forehead.

Eyes and mouths open.
Body stripped down.
But never naked.
Never real.

The day the weights lifted

The gym is closed on my college campus
so, I can't put the same weight on my chest,
can't bench press pass the same pain and pressure,

can't lift
except to lift myself out of bed.

Today my bodyweight is a harder lift.

To act is defined as:
    1) To pretend
    2) To do
    3) A stage of a play, of a story playing out

Of those options
in today's multiple choice
I'm likely choosing the first:

to pretend like loneliness
isn't a heavy shoulder press

as if I'm not squatting down,
hiding from the world

that my abs
don't want to do a single crunch
into a ball
beneath a bed
barely fit upon
much less under.

The campus dining halls remain locked
so, I can't put the same food in my belly,

can't shovel down the same anaesthesia,
can't digest
except to process my own gut feelings
I'd rather ignore.

Today those gut instincts
seem harder to swallow
to shove somewhere
they can't be heard

I should choose Act II:
to "do" pass despair
get up and walk it off
go exercise
the food for thought
that doesn't flow
with my regular diet.

Yet the cold outside
freezes any future sweat
or tears
before they can form,

is frigid about staying put
staying shut in my room
and in my head

no headroom to be driven
in any vehicle of change
no headspace to fit
any thoughts to expand.

It's unlikely the campus library will be open
but technically I am faculty here
technically I should have access

technically I have the faculties
to access an alternative book
with more shelf life than "hide at home."

Ain't I a human being housed in artistry?
In stories, don't most things happen in 3's'?
3 phases
3 stages
3 acts

What about ACT III?:
what if...
at this stage of the play
I was to play freely?

without expectation
without situations
like class
or career

no college tuition
to accredit my spirit
from where my intuition
wishes to muse

to have zero instructions
on how to be responsible
for anyone or anything else
and instead, be able to respond
Authentically in the world

be...Authentically
in the world?

The campus has shut down

but I don't have to.
I can activate my own school of thought
follow what drives me and my rules of the road
only known by this soul

the sole person in the library
who can lift the high piles of book
I've been looking for
that I haven't been able to look within
to uplift my being
alongside my reason for being here.

Today, I'll let the campus stay closed
while I stay open
believing that,
even without a gym
to exercise this moment of despair,
It will still all work out.

G. WIGGINS
UNITED STATES OF AMERICA

BIO

Native American; Retired Paralegal and Certified Public Manager; Love to write; Love the outdoors; Love my husband and family and God.

CONNECT

Facebook @Grace Wiggins
Instagram @gwigster49

CALAMITY

Life can be a disaster, but only if you allow it,
So take your time in reaching ruin.

Do you wake up in the morning wanting to fail?
Or do you make that decision instantaneously?

What makes you think you are the only one?
There are others in the same ship you are.

Paddle up the river of life to reach your success, or
Paddle down the river of life and reach your catastrophe.

Make up your mind soon for life is not guaranteed.
Choose wisely, my friend, for just one chance is given.

To succeed and become whole, is a matter of choice,
That's your discovery to overcome calamity.

RHETORICAL

YOU FIND YOURSELF ASKING WHY,
OR IS IT JUST BECAUSE.

DOES IT REALLY MATTER,
DOES ANYONE CARE.

WHY DON'T YOU JUST STOP,
OR SHOULD WE JUST GO FORWARD.

COULD IT BE THE BEGINNING,
BUT THEN IT COMES TO AN END.

CAN THIS GO ON AND ON,
YEAH, I'M SURE IT CAN AND WILL.

SILENCE

The razor-sharp quietness was deafening,
As I walked through the endless tunnel.
Even the light penetrating through the darkness,
Was without sound.

I reached out to grab the stillness in front of me,
But only felt the hanging emptiness.
My footsteps didn't even have the strength,
To break through the silence.

Continuing the travel through the nothingness,
Felt just like an endless journey.
There wasn't much to see of this space,
Only the blackness before my eyes.

The light in my hands is my only solace,
Knowing it will light my way.
Through this deep darkness that goes on and on,
It takes me to where I will break the silence.

WOUNDED

The pain was agonizing, heart wrenching and brutal.
It was unbearable, but he would have to endure.

For seemingly endless hours following the tragedy, his mind wandered aimlessly, and like cobwebs was profusely entangled.

His saddened heart was like a lead weight heavy in his chest, and he was unwilling to readily accept any compromise for his crushing failure.

And so he ultimately discovered that he could become a viable pawn in life, by surviving the maiming of his being, and not become a helpless bleeding fatality.

FOUR WALLS

Have you ever wondered if the four walls you occupy have a life?
Do they provide you with security and shelter you in times of danger?
Are they always there, standing tall and casting darkened shadows?
Or do you just take it for granted they are empty shells of nothing.
The memories tendered within those walls are forever there, and
Their echoes are loud and can never be silenced.
You are part of those four walls as you live through all the emotions,
And all the experiences oozing out of you to cover every corner.
There is life in those walls, they speak to you if you just listen.

CATS

Felines are not a man's best friend, they stand alone.
They accept you, and not you, them.
Give them a pat on the head, and they look at you sideways.
Stroke them down their back, and they long for more.
They wrap themselves around your feet, wanting more.
Tolerance is part of their demeanour, and they show you how it is.
If they want you in their lives, they provide you with all the signs,
And if you think you are dominant over them, you will be disappointed.
It is their choice to be with you, they provide you with presents,
And if you find a bird, a lizard, or a mouse on your doorstep,
You have been accepted.

AZARIA CAMARGO
AUSTRALIA

BIO

Azaria Camargo (she/her) is a slightly unhinged wordsmith of dark poetry and prose. She hopes to evoke wonder, curiosity and discomfort through her work and encourage society to fall back in love with reading and the literary arts. When Azaria isn't dreaming of new ways to disturb readers, she enjoys caring for her pet chickens and ducks at her humble home in Melbourne, Australia.

CONTEXT FOR POEMS

'One of three' and 'Wildwood Dancing' are expressions of chaotic love and sapphic adoration penned by Azaria Camargo. While there are elements of storytelling that draw inspiration from Azaria's personal experiences, both texts are intended to be interpreted freely by readers.

CONNECT
Facebook @azariaacamargo
Instagram @azariacamargo

One of three
Originally published in Dark Winter Literary Magazine (July 2023)

I have no memorable sexual experiences with you.
You were only just okay.

Surely, we must have cared for one another
We gave each other one of our lifetimes, freely.
      Deeply, emotionally – but definitely not happily!
No veils nor embellishments
It was an awful hot mess.
Tolerating each other while
Tracing raw flesh, tasting intimate instruments
Never consummating

Funnily enough, you are one of three
That I have supposedly ever loved.
So, it's quite sad is it not?
When I'm reminded of your existence
      Hypocrisy
      Paranoia
      Adversarial exchanges
That is all that I can recall

Why did you find it morally necessary
To embark on an extremist, pessimistic path?

How did you become my one of three
That I ever loved
When I cannot find any kind words for you

Ah! There is one influential thing
I am dying to purge from my spirit

Your constant manifestos about Death.

Before you stained my contentment
I rarely gave it much thought
                    To you
Death was not the end. Even worse
Upon death we will meet our Creator
Unwillingly receiving judgement for all our ill decisions

I respectfully disagree. But suddenly
        Death has festered
A contagion in my mind I cannot shake
One day I will be gone.
My identity and entirety instantly inconsequential
Meaningless atoms to be repurposed by the universe.

You are one of three.
Eventually, you will become nothing.
        As will I.

Wildwood Dancing
Originally published in T'Art Winter Showcase (November 2023)

She was golden ferned.
       And golden aged
Jubilee differences
Shared sapphic struggles

A dance of discreet dialogues
Sometimes about her
Sometimes about me
Occasionally about nonsense

She fearlessly freed me of
A thorny lilac crown
The kiss of her familiar petals
Scattered across a supple surface.

                        then
'My husband and I have reconciled.'
                        No matter.

Somehow someone adored me
Tended to my roots
       a broken hot mess.

Holding safe in my heart
Our secret strelitzia
Unearthed from her velvet black dress.

When he got mad
Originally published in Dark Winter Literary Magazine (July 2023)

When he got mad
Suddenly and quickly
We are worthless

Not wanting to overstep
Lola and *Lolo* rush home
Like me, pretending not to hear
Bruises being birthed

In limbo we live as ghosts
Consuming our wrongdoings

We deserve it
To suffer in silence for days
He was tired. We were jovial
As lesser beings, we had
      no right

Sometimes. When he got mad
My tiny hand shakily dialled 000
Terrified of breaking my father's heart
I hung up each time.

When you get mad I wonder
How did you come
      to know my unworthiness too?

Letters to the ghost seeker

Remember when
You and I were the best of friends?

In a deluded dream
We bonded while I was with another
My broken keys full of wanting
To be enraptured
Seen
By a chosen brother.

Untimely, I realise now
I was selfish – hideously selfish.
A budding narcissist.
You absorbed of all my dreams
My troubles and secrets

I ignored that you too had battles,
And so much more.
Musical aspirations
A beaten but open heart

After all of your challenges,
You could still be immersed
Completely and deeply
In an ultimate love

'I am not a child,
I know what love is.'
The real child couldn't believe you
My insecurities, immaturity
Subservience to family
Addiction to an addicted other
All these petty and pointless things

After lifetimes spent apart
Reborn through epic journeys
Heartbroken by other lovers,
We always found our way back
Still enamoured with one another.

Dialogues of honesty and sadness
During discrete reunions
Intimate tracing of the stars
You always the listener
I always the taker

And of course
The spontaneous *ménage à quatre*
Never had I felt so close to you.
Finally, we were ready

To venture on the construct, we danced around
Always deferred, always unneeded
Until finally, it seemed like it was.
'Let's be in a relationship.'

We already shared delusions
We overcame shared conflict

And now this was it.
Nothing could go wrong.

Struck suddenly and too young
The universe stole your mentor of music
Grief unearthed other feelings
For her.
My friend.
      Your other ghost.

Space, support, and a stretch of time
The natural and necessary trinity.
I was aware but had no capacity it seemed

'I will always be here for you, as your friend.'
I thought I meant it in earnest.
As I waltzed away
As the taker but never the giver, once again.

'I will always have a soft spot for you'
You had said
When we were platonic once again.
I hope those sentiments are still true
The chaos had come to an end

On most days, I'm happy for you.

Do I regret that you've likely forgotten when
You and I were the best of friends?

      Admittedly, I really could not say.

Though I miss it when your fingers
Mastered music in my body.
Tenderly
Often,
    Adagio.
In that special climatic way.

JONA ESELAYE DAVID
AUSTRALIA

BIO

Jona Eselaye David (she/her) is a new voice from Melbourne, Australia with an educational background in Applied Science (Biotechnology) and Business Management. She enjoys consuming and creating edgy or witty works with a touch of fantasy. As an emerging children's author, Jona also writes whimsical stories to encourage a love for literature in younger readers. After almost ten years of building a career as a professional in the higher education sector, Jona decided to continue her professional development through vocational studies. She is currently studying Professional Writing and Editing.

CONTEXT FOR POEMS

Jona weaved together 'This Forest' and 'Hunger' after a ten-year hiatus from writing. The fantasy elements and gritty tone of 'This Forest' was inspired by Jona's favorite childhood fantasy junior fiction series. This piece became Jona's debut in the global poetry world when it was published in Ascend by Hearth and Coffin Literary Journal (Volume 3, Issue 2).

CONNECT
Facebook @jonaedavid
Instagram @jonadavid.writer
www.linkedin.com/in/jonadavid
www.linktr.ee/jonadavid

Hunger

All art is useless / Oscar Wilde had rightly said
Yet I'm hungry for minds to weave new worlds
Where unseen souls are dancing denizens
Undefined by their ugly truths or glossy pearls

      Do you share my hunger
Or are you content with what culture has become?
Do you consume, envy and hope?
All the petty things in which you've chosen to succumb

Critically endangered are the starving artists
The corporate clones of their former selves
Old relics
      once rich in life
Decompose on forgotten ghostly shelves

Curated claims for generic modern norms
Sell illusions dressed as spiritual healing.
Yet now we need all dialogues to be literal
Because we are consuming, never feeling.

Pipers - outrageous, ornate or odd
Whisper wonders the world may never learn
Those songs are simply no longer fashionable
Unlike dazzles adorned by friends we greenly yearn

Travellers transformed by poetry are no more
Because metaphors require some effort to understand
Come the first spring we embark for easy, rapid wins
To collect branded goods and rendered abodes of grand

How many idol lifestyles with facades did you fund?
Wealthy from the admiration you were willing to give.

Because while you consumed, envied and hoped
You forgot that you had a life of your own to live.

My hunger searches for discarded dreams
So that before our souls are too far dead
We can help ourselves remember
All those beautiful, useless things
        That our hearts can feel instead.

This Forrest
Originally published in Hearth and Coffin Literary Magazine (July 2023)

      There is no doubt.
This forest is a dark and frightening place.

But among the monsters survives a girl.
Where ghastly creatures thrive and defend their home
She is unkept, unremembered and unloved
No matter. For here, she is all alone.

Strangely, for earthly monsters she has no fear,
Now she's learned the song of silence can be serene.
Hushed are the howls of hunted strangers,
Crimson spatters in a wonderful world of green.

She may never know, that once
She was a daughter destined for forge and fire.
Identity and protection, loaned out of loyalty
Then stolen by nameless men of steel attire.

Ancient foliage protects the shelter
A precious inked bear tucked away
Broken chattels and a crafted jewelled dagger
The only treasured relics from before that cursed day.

When she's a woman
She may begin to wonder
The bluestone palace and humble village
Merely a traveller's walk south yonder.

Would she return to the corrupt citadel
That her parents had been so willing to flee?
Accept that for the final battle, her origins

Are still where she is expected to be?

Mazes of strange places.

In which she could start her life anew.
Then her scars a stern reminder,
Only this forest will welcome her home.
After all, isn't she a monster too?

TERRICA STRUDWICK
AUSTRALIA

I acknowledge the Gangulu people of the land in which I was born. I give my respect to my own and all ancestors past present and for future generations to walk this beautiful world.

BIO

All my life I have found solace in nature. I have mostly lived in small towns throughout regional and rural Australia. I currently live in a historical town in the Northern Flinders Ranges with a population of around 15 people.

It is the most peaceful country I have ever been on, and I very much appreciate the differences between living a very simple life versus the modern-day luxuries such as running hot water and flushing toilets and the privilege I have, I choose to live between the two.

CONTEXT FOR POEMS

Mother Earth is my inspiration for life. The poems I have contributed revolve around our inherent connection to Nature and the parallels we can draw between our lives and the elements, seasons and cycles on Earth.

Nature helps me to make sense of my inner worlds, the world we live in and my place in it. Writing, for me, opens gateways to process my emotions and feelings. It allows me to witness and see the polarities that exist within us and in Nature, and how systems will always try to maintain balance and harmony. Writing provides me with peace, calm and inspiration to consistently grow and become a better human in an ever-changing world.

Initiation

A sacred journey that those before
Have taken a thousand times over,
Across every shore.
The waves, the ocean, move with her core.

Women have held this knowledge most assured,
The rites of passage,
The paths of initiation,
Upon each who chooses to walk with her.

An invitation to the beloved,
Inanna, Ishtar, Isis, Aphrodite,
Venus.
She rises as the morning star.

She whispers and caresses your most sacred vessel,
Holding within her the holy flame,
As you release your innermost hidden ghosts,
In the perfect form that they may take.

Breathe in her beauty, take her all in,
What is within is always without,
Allow her to have you without any doubt,
Her love and beauty is yours to claim.

I am within what I see without,
What I see without is what I am within,
The greatest and most delightful testimony,
To beautiful Venus and our Moon.

With or without you knowing,
She brings treasures for you all around,
Look in the mirror and be kind,
What you are searching for, you will find.

Listen

Her bones scattered upon the ground,
The wind howls like the cries of our ancestors,
And we weep in sorrow,
For all that has been,
And forsaken on this sacred land.

Her tears form rivers and wash into streams,
Bringing life to what was once hollow,
Laid bare, naked, reborn.
Passion and gold running through her veins.

She opens her eyes to see,
A new purpose to fulfill,
Sweeping the land with her heartfelt prayers,
To bring balance and harmony for others to share.

Sitting in silence, she speaks to you,
Sending sweet whispers on the fall of a feather.
Listen very quietly, as deep as you can,
And move in her seasons and cycles.

Embody her rhythms within,
A hum.
A buzz, that only she can bring.

Be Still

Be still.
Her beating heart calls,
Through the winds it breaks,
All chords and attachments.

The planets move,
Mercury and Mars,
Calling us to release, release, release.
The tethers come down,
The veils are lifted,
And I can see once more,
Exactly where I pay my intentions,
Of a fulfilling and joyful life.

Spreading my wings,
I fly and don't fall... I said I fly and don't fall.
The birds watch on as eyes,
For the Ancestors,
Exalting in awe with renewed hope,
They too fly and soar,
Across the skies,
The bridge between worlds.

Be still,
She calls.
Be still and soar.

The Ancient Land

Sensing sirens from within,
The black heart softens
And turns to grains of sand.
She smiles and feels her power.

She is.
Present, Being, Conscious.
Aware of her deep alchemy
Taking place within.

She knows her name,
It whispers on the birdsong.
It carries on the winds of change.
Gently sweeping over mountains and rocky terrain.

This landscape of hers is vast,
She knows it very well,
Like she's been here before.
An ancient land she calls home.

Sweeping views, a horizon seen from
Anywhere on the land.
Nothing is hidden here.
A place to lay your soul bare…

Witness to itself.
All of my parts are welcome,
And I call them back to me.
Hello my loves, are you ready?

Woman

Women gathering with bare feet,
Stomping the ground to a natural beat,
A beat so ancient, it's in their bones.
Dancing together on our sacred Mother.

They weave, they ebb and they flow,
To her deep rhythm under toe.
Drawing her energy up, it rises,
Breathing fire into their beautiful tummies.

She activates their creative womb space,
The divine feminine within, their destiny awaits.
The energy keeps rising up to their hearts
The feelings of freedom, where do we start?

Expanding the feeling of absolute pleasure,
Filling their whole body with unconditional love,
The feeling of expansion is self assured
Longing is lost, and love is sent back for all.

The women are dancing,
The excitement builds,
And they let out a roar!
To reclaim their voices once more.

The memories return,
Their connection to nature awakens the call,
To sit and deeply listen for what may speak,
Shining gifts for them to explore.

With intuitive guidance from within,
Feet firmly planted, grounded, and strong,
The women connected at heart as one,
They open and trust their connection to all.

From deep, deep within Mother Nature's core,
To the boundless worlds of space and furthermore,
They are suspended, supported, and protected,
To now fly free in their own embrace.

Dream

Don't call yourself a Mother.
Don't call yourself a Queen.
Don't call yourself a fighter,
When you are just a dream.

A really, really bad one...
One where you're the beast and I'm the queen!
Fallen far from your race,
To a complete and utter disgrace.

You make me hurl mountains,
And I feel like I'm in chains.
Spanning across the great barren plains,
Laid bare for the birds to peck.

I lay in agony, awaiting my death,
Knowing choices must be made,
To see to it that the sun will fade.
Sunk deep in the earth, silently asleep.

Swirling in darkness in sacred keep,
The wind howls above,
And beckons me back.
It demands that I get back on track.

So claim yourself as Mother.
Claim yourself as Queen.
Claim yourself as a fighter,
And don't ever, ever forget to dream.

Destined

The crackling of the fire
And my love for you
Reaches beyond the enons of time
Immortal
Meandering through lifetimes
We were destined to meet
It is like a full belly
Upon a delicious meal
The smell of the ocean
In the early evening waves
The sight of your eyes
When it's been so long
That smell of vanilla and
Rose with silver enclosed
I'm sure you don't quite know
How much you glow
With wisdom and gold
Inside every atom
In every thread
Through the fabric of time
We dance back together
Through Venus and the Moon

She Speaks

She speaks through the wind
Gentle whispers caress my body
Awakening
The deep stirrings of my soul

She speaks in whispers
Awakening
Some deeper part of me
Breath in

My body relaxes and I move
With her essence
Deep inside I feel her calling
Breath out

Calling for my soul to be free
Free to be me
Fiercely Me
As she moves all around me

SKYE PRICE
ENGLAND, UK

BIO

Skye Price has used poetry as a guide through her life, so she decided to learn it, teach it, and write it. Skye lives and breathes poetry as a Secondary English Teacher and a graduate of a creative writing masters.

Skye lives in the countryside, where she draws inspiration from the nature around her. This has seen her work published in a variety of anthologies such as open-door magazine, ripple, and dream well publishing.

CONNECT
TikTok @poemsandplaces
Instagram @skyepricepoetry

It all happened too quickly

One day I was
asking if you were ok,
the next, the answer
was too obvious for the question,
you could say we had warning
but I disagree
you didn't slip gracefully,
you fell suddenly
and couldn't get back up.

Sometimes I could bring you back
with the song that used to move you
around the kitchen, your eyes following
the pattern of younger footsteps,
singing so full of heart in the same room
where I saw you forget the
sound of your own voice, of mine.

The melody was not loud enough
to serve as a permanent anchor,
as your eyes became stiller
and stiller, and the tune drifted
until it was just a song
'a pretty song'
that someone might sing to,
if they knew the words.

A Touch of Gold

What once sat barely noticed on kitchen counters,
used occasionally and put back away,
fell from its place and across the icy tiles.
A fractured, hopeful face was found in the chaos
that fragmented on the floor. Its lonely
eyes demanded it be glued together with the echoes
of its grief. It begged to be believed,
that shattered pieces still have worth.

One by one, she nimbly hand-picked the shards,
examining how each edge had split away
from the last. She could brush it up swiftly,
and move on with her day, but she just couldn't
ignore the stranded eyes and splintered smile
that longed for someone to see
that shattered pieces still have worth.

Radiant rivers dripped through the cracks
with a steady, patient hand. Time blew a cool wind
into each vain, as it dried the walls together.
It's shining wounds drenched in gold, spilling
through unpredictable trails.
When left optionless, you're forced to see
That shattered pieces still have worth.

It blinked itself awake, looking
as though it were designed this way;
hiding in the clay, waiting for someone brave
enough to pick apart its seamless façade
and uncover a soul much more striking.
Now that it sits there so miraculously, it's clear
That shattered pieces still have worth.

She looked at it and smiled.

"You are a work of art."

The Gardener

Square edges meticulously meet at 90 degrees
Refusing to jut outside of its assigned boundaries
Each blade of grass is cut to the exact same height
In a still sea of emeralds; clones cut from a single blade

This lawn feels like a marshmallow carpet
Under your feet, it bounces, so healthily,
Like memory foam. If you tread lightly enough,
Spreading your weight evenly, it could teach you to hover

The metal gardener, with its sapphire lit eyes
And iron smile, paces the garden in perfect repetition
Holding its traditions in the pre-programmed route
It stamps out day after day after day

Each arm holds seamlessly curved blades
Which rock back and forth, snipping so
Minutely that the wind sweeps away the clippings
Back and forth and back and forth

Some of the residents effortlessly time their pathways;
Some become obstacles, torn down with the same
Focussed expression looking straight
Through the floating skin confetti

Spliced and sprinkled onto the lawn
The foundations squelch awake and
Slurp up the clotted liquid, seeping through
The blades and nourishing the soil

What a beautiful garden

Firefly

Fireflies fly free
Unaware of the light trail they leave

Tiny fleeting flickers in time
Catching the attention of bewildered eyes

Suspended like fairy lights in the night
Radiating hope without a cause

You don't even know the smiles you've brightened
Tiny, wonderful, buzzing orbs

When the world catches fire
And the waters rise

I hope they leave us the fireflies

Ferocious

Her world was dipped in fire
Soaked in molten lava
Every natural disaster
Surged one after the other

She held onto the anger
It was a gnawer and a biter
Claws out, gripping tighter
Vomit up the trauma

Words spat out in bile
Her insides settle stale
She did not light the match
But, she nurtured the flames so well.

Working Wings

She flew like she was born with working wings
Sprouting them for the strength of her spine
The flurry of the air through mountains sing

Years spent grounded, soles of feet blackening
Soul burning out in monotonous heat
She flew like she was born with working wings

In brick laid streets, she's been lingering
Now, she wishes to be where it's grown fresh from soil
The flurry of the air through mountains sing

In an unobstructed sunrise, she sheds her skin
Bleeds out the concrete and soaks in the hues
She flew like she was born with working wings

Miles of land that no one owns is beckoning
Finding worth in its serenity, not its price
The flurry of air through the mountains sing

The chains that held her are lay amongst piles of things
Things she does not need now she's found her feathers
She flew like she was born with working wings
The flurry of air through the mountains sing

JANE RICHARDS
SCOTLAND, UK

BIO

Jane is an avid writer and animal lover. With a debut picture book coming out, she has been eager to turn her hand to another literary passion - poetry. Jane writes about the walks of life she has encountered in her 32 years of growing up in bonnie Scotland.

By The Water's Edge

By the water's edge, a calm place to be.
Crowds gather in winter winds.
Three bridges span three generations
Community spirit lights the shore.

By the water's edge, giving is all year round
Random acts of kindness are the norm
Painted stones and coastal homes
Pawprints glisten in the snow

By the water's edge, eyes gaze upwards
Explosive colours fill the skies
Murals and gardens kept by kind souls
Treasured memories built to last

By the water's edge Weddings, well wishes and friends
Community food and prayer
A stranger stops to check you're not lonely
Possessions gifted and shared

By the waters edge, ships bring visitors many
In awe of such beauty and welcoming
Charity and hope glow bright
As festivities roll into the night

By the water's edge, a well trodden track
As carriages trundle over the bridge.
Dreamy views while coffee brews
At the station where it all begins

By the water's edge, shop local, please do!
Supporting one another

Market fairs and talents bloom
Pints raised in celebration

A community by the water are we
The Ferry, the place to be.

The Woodland

Huddling underneath the canopy,
The water-logged clouds pass by.
Bird song and salty sea air raise his spirits,
As he waits to catch the ideal shot.

Too much to see, butterflies and more.
To one side lies an industrial cavern,
With a backdrop of blue crystal waters.
A grand fortress lies to the other side,
The stark contrast revealing a history of economic difference
Along one coastline.

Passers-by jog in the rain, no sign they even notice,
A friendly nod, as the clouds begin to part.
The floodlit path now glistening,
The darkened woods are even more inviting in contrast.

Camera round neck, he makes his way to the woods.
Hearing rustling through the bush, squirrels chasing tails above.
Would the perfect moment present itself today?
What does a perfect shot look like anyway?

Further and further away into the woodlands, the coast disappears.
As he disappears into his own mind, down the forgiving trail.
All sense of direction and time lost,
Every direction is a perfect frame of imagery.

Fairytale mushrooms, dewdrops and canopy shadows,
An otherworldly sense of peace.
He closes his eyes and snaps blindly into the woods,
Letting the atmosphere be his guide.

Opening his eyes, in the distance he saw

A couple holding hands.
Framed by the shrubbery, a picture-perfect scene,
But not perfect by all means.

He looked carefully at the pictured he took blindly,
Smiling down at the imperfect composition.
Slightly out of focus,
A true reflection of the world for many.

Leaving the woods, the sun began to set.
With a sense of purpose, he began along the coast,
Instead of the castle, he made towards the industrial estate,
In seek of the images which go unseen.

The Bridge

Lashes of rain rolled through the sky like a taunting matador
Beckoning her into a faultless world which would lead to peril

The bridge was her canopy, her unwavering shield
Which she battled with every day

Headlights and laughter passed above her
The waterlogged and stagnant soil her chosen stable ground

Friendly faces of rats and stray cats a welcome sight
Company has no standards to meet here, only a heartbeat

She left only when she had to, to find food
Taken, never paid for. She would make it up to them some day.

She would pay it forward, any kindness given
Feeding leftover scraps to pigeons or the scraggly felines

There were never really "leftovers".
She would go a little hungry.

"You can't live here little girl" is all she would hear
Offers of shelter or to be taken to the police

Warm hearts, untarnished minds. Never tainted by cruelty
Unlike her. She was glad they couldn't understand.

Who would feed the friendly faces if she left?
What life would lie at the other end of the bridge?

Would it keep her dry and warm at night?
Would she have company?
Stability?

Each day was the same for her there, staring into the matador
A backwards merry go round in black and white

But when she woke every morning with the sun peeking over the bridge.

She was home

STEPHANIE ROWE

(MRS ROWE)

AUSTRALIA

BIO

Embark on a journey into the vibrant tapestry of my life, where each moment is an adventure waiting to unfold. I thrive on the richness of experiences, living life to its fullest.

I have written since I could hold a pen and connected to my consciousness, I have boxes of journals from all over my life where I have scribbled down poetry or song lyrics. Short stories from my vivid and lively imagination, which span across my lifetime. The Arts hold a special place in my heart, I put on a multi arts festival in 2010 in Brisbane called "Live to Shine", where I had musicians, performers, circus and visual artists participate. I am proactively a participant in the arts wherever I am at the time, my driving force has always been bringing people together while giving opportunities and guidance.

I have most recently released my self-published memoir "Fiercely ME". I have orchestrated, organized and published the fruition of this poetry book "The Worlds In Our Words". I anticipate I will continue this poetry collaboration as an annual release going forward.

My passion for connection is a cornerstone of my existence. Together with my husband, Jason, we merge the joys of bringing people together and the artistry of cooking. Our culinary escapades span the globe, from the Caribbean to the Philippines and the Mediterranean, weaving nights filled with love, laughter, and profound connections with our nearest and dearest.

Fresh from a six-month odyssey across Europe and South America (November 2023), my husband, Jason, and I have returned with a profound understanding of ourselves. Each country became a classroom, and we eagerly absorbed the diverse lessons embedded in their cultures. The journey was more than a physical exploration; it was a deep dive into self-discovery, a transformative experience that enriched our lives in ways we never imagined. The liberty to experience life fully and connect with our surroundings is a privilege we don't take lightly. Natural hot springs became our sanctuaries, leading us to serene and beautiful corners of the world.

From the tender age of youth, poetry has been my chosen form of expression. Whether captivating audiences at events and spoken word nights, including Queensland Poetry, or delivering speeches infused with warmth and wisdom, my words resonate on both professional and personal fronts. The ability to intrigue and captivate is an art I've honed.

Dedication has forged my success. As I create the extraordinary life and business of my dreams, my love for humanity takes center stage in everything. Join me on this transformative journey, where every word, every adventure, is a testament to the power of living authentically and with purpose.

CONNECT
Facebook @Mrs-Rowe-Author
Instagram @mrs_rowe_author
TikTok @stephannierowe
www.mrsrowe.org

Mexican Sun

Your days shine deep within my soul,
Warming me, from the inside out,
You touch the earth,
With your golden rays,
Creating a masterpiece,

Time, stood, still,
As I savoured, every moment,
Burnt into my memory,
Forever to be held in my heart,
Cascading down over the green, rolling hills,
With prickly pears dotted everywhere,
As if someone blew them over the land,
The trickle of life,
The creek slowly runs over the stones,

Humans carve into the white stone,
Like we own the land.
We are just the caretakers.

The land soothes the soul,
Relinquishing to its power,
In return, taking my pain,
Selflessly.
Mexican sun gives life, but it can also take it.
Nature balancing act, the bookie of life.
Prickles lay across the land, warding off survival.
Humans can be just as prickly,

Mexico soothes my soul,
The pain you take, also is given,
I feel your pain in the same breath,
I see the dirt all over your body,

Exhaustion covers your face,
As you fall asleep on the rock wall,
The sun beating down on us all,
I wish, I could shade you from the sun,
The smell of dust never leaves your soul.
Mexico, my love affair.
I will always love you.

A Glimpse of Life Itself

Time stood still,
As I floated, in between life, and death,

My body in mid-air, as if gravity didn't exist,

A feeling which I never knew I needed to feel,
Time stopped,

As I floated,

Is my mind playing tricks?
Smash,
The force of the car hitting the earth,

Everything crumbled,

The sensation of falling,
Over lapping, like a life on repeat,
This time gravity had come to play,
Not realising how fragile life was until I felt it disappear,

Chaos, as the world tumbled around me,

Questioning everything, in moments which felt like lifetimes,

Am I real?
Is this real?
Am I really going to die here?

As my mind came back to my body,

I couldn't understand why I survived,
Why we had survived,

The Amazon doesn't take hostages, it rebirths life,
As I lay in the carnage of broken glass and spirits,
All I could think was,

You tried, to kill me,
And failed,

As the luscious green leaves floated down through the air,
I thought,
We are atoms that survive by the glimpse of reaction,

I lay staring through the opening of my soul,
What will be,
Will be,
But this is my life to succeed.

Albania

The ticking of the electricity lines makes a rhythmic noise to the mind.

Smokey haze surrounding the world, I have chosen to be in.

The crack of the gears and the crunch of the rocks as the cars drive by,
Over and over again, like a horror movie you can't escape from.

While life darts back and forth across the white line.

The sun looks like a sci fi film, and we are waiting for the day we incinerated by its rays.

A corn field is pebbles throw away while we step back in time.

Towering over it is a hotel, all shiny and new.

The stray dog so sad a reflection of the countries people, desperate to survive, dirt surrounding life.

I wish life was different, but I know that tomorrow won't bring any relief.

A sad and angry country filled with old men crinkled from the sun pulling their donkeys through the traffic.

You really do step into another dimension here.

RAGE The dark hole we never speak of

My soul oozes like the skies in monsoonal season,
Raining, pouring, flooding.

Thunder bellowing from my mouth.
My heart races.

Fidgeting,
My breath, no longer my own,

My body drenched in adrenaline,
My hands shake as I realise,
I am a passenger to my body,

I feel the fire, start in my torso,
A match to fuel, engulfing my body,
The takeover was unstoppable,
I was never going to stop it,

A familiar feeling,
The darkness, we never like to talk about,
Exists nevertheless, coming out from the shadows,

The relief pouring over my body, like a cold shower on a summer day,
I let go, submitting to the treachery,
I know which will come,
A passenger watching the carnage unfold,
As my rage devours those in my path,
I leave no hostages.

Can I come back?
Will I come back?

I feel the hot blood coursing through my veins, a savage for the adrenaline.

I am gone.
A shadow in the background,

Quietly whimpering,
Hoping the courage, I need will return,
To stop the beast,
The angry raging beast,

Rage,

Covers my organs like cancer.
I feel the suffocation, even if I am alive
My light being strangled, still fighting to be alive.

The coldness, chills the soul,
I will return,
But not now,
Now I fall,
Into the abyss of life,

Delphi

I close my eyes and breath in,
A direct connection to a world we cannot see,
Can be felt,
Your presence still lingers in the air,
You were here.

As if the magic is falling all around us,
The smell of pine laced with ancestor's souls,
We are in the centre of the universe,
A witness to the creation, of life,

The light touches the world as if it was made only for my eyes.

I feel the earths heartbeat,
The heat bubbles inside of me,
The hard rock surface, an attempt of deterrent,
A visual force for the mind,
The water laps at edges of the universe, all encompassing,
Attempting to cool our souls,
While the heat still generates inside us,
Turmoil between the worlds,
The implosion of us can be seen from afar,
As we try to destroy, by collapsing,
The centre of the universe is straight down.
You just need to look.
I watch on, as if the ending of the would be different.

The seasons come and go while life clashes, life is passed on and continues the survival
Unsure what the survival is for.

The Stonemason:

The Stonemason was great at building walls so much so that people would come from all over the world to admire his masterpieces, even if it was to keep people out, there was a beauty to the way he enclosed life.

I asked the stonemason if he could show me how to build my own wall.
The stonemason patiently showed me how to create a sturdy wall filled with intricate beauty.
I decided one day that it was time that I build my own wall, not just any wall but a wall to enclose my heart.

Brick by brick I enclosed my heart making a fierce unbreakable wall, I was building it with my bare hands, with every brick I lay was a tear never to be felt again, for every brick I lay was sadness I would never feel again, for every stone that I lay was a reminder to me of a heart ache never to be felt.

Knowing that the closure of my heart was the only way forward I didn't stop until the wall was finished.

I could feel the shiver of winter touching my core and as I layered up to keep warm, I could still feel the bitter cold, the cold took no hostages.

I felt the wall quiver, *ca boom, ba ba boom*, went the beating of my heart, I could feel that her heart was alone, shut off from the world, my heart was trying desperately to escape from the wall which surrounded it.

I looked up to the sky; it was black like the night, the wind blowing as if it controlled the world. I stood there listening to my heart beating.

I felt the pulse run through my neck as if lightening had struck me. The wind entangled my body wanting to pull me in every direction; I couldn't stop it, I fell into its grasp.

The rain pouring uncontrollable I looked down at my feet the water rising engulfing my feet, until there was nothing left except my head bobbing in the water. The mud entrenched me, my feet no longer my own stuck in thickness, which would not let go; it refused to let me move. The day had come, the day to free my heart.

I called upon my stonemason, friend, will you help me break my heart free? The stonemason replied, "of course I will," he disappeared returning with his chisel in hand.

For each moment I wanted to hide away to never feel again, to deprive myself of lust, of love and touch, broke my heart.

He broke the wall away brick by brick, chiseling each brick with precision, with every brick removed was releasing my heart to feel again, harmony with the external world, the purest part of being human, to feel again.

For every moment I never wanted to love again, refusing to feel, turning away from feeling he chiseled a little more away. There was a moment of release my heart pumping in life being filled up and invigorated with every feeling, sensation and desire, the stonemason had released my heart from the secure wall which deprived it from life. To feel again, to cherish the moments in life we dream of could be felt once more.

The stonemason was a kind soul, and he ever so gently freed me from my own wall, I realised the storm had subsided, the sun was poking through the clouds shining down on my face, the only thing left to do was to continue on my journey. I will forever be indebted to the stonemason, the man who so patiently freed my heart/ wall

The world, spins around you. . . . .

I wake,
The feeling hits me,
I feel crushed,
The weight of, my, mind,
It has, begun,
It never stopped,

The vortex,
Between dream and consciousness,
The feeling of being ripped apart,
From,
Two worlds,
My heart beats,
Uncontrollably,
Reminding me,
I can't escape,

Life pounding like an earthquake,
The reminder of reality,
Pulsating through you,

Like thunder barrelling down, shaking you to the core.
Innocence stripped from you,
Unrecognisable, to the reflection in the mirror,

The feeling of warm, salty tears,
Dripping, onto my chest,

I lie in soft soothing sheets,
Softness touching my skin,
The beautiful illusion of being safe, a cloak disguising life.

I berry myself in menial tasks,

The illusion of distraction,
Will take the pain away,

Well,
They say so anyway,

I create to do lists,
Ticking things off, as easily as they come,
Realising to do lists aren't going to take away the reality you face,
Ain't going to stop me tryin',
As I put another menial task on the list,

The implosion of my strength,
Like a howling wind which fades away,
As if water stopped running,
Rain stopped dropping,
I disintegrate,
As quickly as paper on fire,

I wash myself trying to remove the stain of your experience,
Realising you can't wash away your memories,
Trying to remove your existence again and again,
It never works,
It is your memory,
Like oil on the ocean,

The panic is unsettling,
The emotions uncontrollable,
A Sunami crashing into me

I surrender to the carnage

I have looked into the eyes of fear,
Pierced into my soul,
A reminder of what exists,

I have nothing left to give, I can only burn,
I have seen into the eyes of men who are evil,
No soul,
Only living flesh,

Men who overpower a child,
The joy it brings them is vile,
When you see the eyes of evil,
You have already met with destiny,

The panic,
The fight for life,

As the world spins around you like nothing is happening,
The suffocation, I can't breathe, my breath taken from my small body,
You are alive but the feeling of near death is so close you invite it for tea,

Life,
What life I scream,

My mind turns on me,
The stench of life I was incapable of surviving,

What now?
What have I left to give?
Who am I?
Why am I still alive?
Who do I want to be?

Am I a victim?

What does this all mean?
Screw you, memory,

My treat was to live through it.
My body overcome with tingling,
My chest as tight as guitar string,
I can't string a sentence together,

Sleepwalking through life,
Sleeping is just as versatile as being awake.

Rage,
The rage of a women in the world,
Is like a fire storm engulfing the air around it,
Spitting out crumbs to the wind,

You think I am done,
I won't be done until, I say,
Unstoppable rage which lives inside of me
I sit in the middle feeding it, living in it,

My safe place.

Feeling secure,
No one can touch me in this sphere of rage.
Anger and blood.
The relief as I sit in this place.

I, will, burn, this, world, down and rise as phoenix to the sun,
You thought I died,
I did,
Now I rebirth myself in my own eyes,
With my beating heart,

You can never touch me again, I am fiercely mine to rule.

When I die

When I die,
I want to be burned, cremated.

My life was filled with phoenix moments,
Shattered and incinerated.

Many times.

Always to rise again.

So, when I die, I won't rise again,
I would like to fly, to be free.

Let me go, by the oceans shore,
So, I can swim with the currents.

Let me go, on a windy day,
So, I can fly to the tips of the mountains.

Let me go, on a riverbank,
So, I wash down with the river's current.

Let me go, on top of a hill,
So, I can fly high with the birds, soaring with the winds.

Let me go, in the rainforest,
So, I can grow with the trees.

Life has been tough but o so sweet.

Let me be free,
With the wild earth, to be free for eternity.

Wobbly parts

He loves my thighs,
All my wobbly parts,
He loves my smile
Sees my spirit shine through,
He sees me, he respects me.

He loves my grey hair and all the wrinkles,
The wisdom which I share.

He loves me even when I am crying.
He holds my hand and reassures me of his presence,
He loves me when I don't love myself
His love fuels me into action.

I know you love me.

The wait was worth every moment, the day I met you,
The sparks ignited,
The souls infused,
Care we share grows with every day.

You are the man of my universe who I love with every atom of my soul.

I didn't realise I needed you,
You are a part of my life you are a part of my soul.

COLLABORATIVE POEM:

A POEM FROM 22 POETS TO THE WORLD

This last poem was a project in itself. Stephanie Rowe has driven every creative aspect of *The World In Our Words*. She asked that each poet contribute 2 lines. There was no theme or structure, the poet did not know what the other poet had written. This poem was organically created, and it was up to the poet to write from heart.

Twenty-two poets merged in synchronicity to create this beautiful poem. It is testament to the entire project of this book where each author had a voice in the progression from start to finish. It is a testament to unite people regardless of all the challenges facing humanity. We hope to inspire people all around to free themselves of barriers, nationalities, languages, ideologies to come together through the power words. We hope you enjoy this poem as much as we have creating it.

The words are worlds in themselves, where the "L" is not about losing
But instead choosing to lose ourselves in them.
As the sun rises and the waves flow.
my thoughts and wonders are combined.
Brave hearts open to feel the motions of life's flow.
Sometimes may be challenging but the strength to survive shines bright in the darkness.
The wind blows ragged gasps and joyful sighs across hillside and sea.
Stirring the remains of all that came before and all that still will come to be.
Life is fragile, just like new buds on the tree.
Awakening in the sunlight to a new beginning.
Words escape the fate of all that remains untold.
Stories for the ages as futures unfold.
The haunting endures.
Carried through lifetimes grown apart.
Epic journeys to know another.
Satiated and content,
Domesticated. Playing house.
        but still enamoured
        with that ghostly other
A lover of solitude am I - of mountain heights, of ocean depths, of space.
So limitless that nothingness decrees it for its own.

I now know that I can be brave.
I will face this world head-on and revel in all of its terrifying beauty.
Come around river, let hope surround the sorrow…
…like a whisper sighing for the moon; embracing the wind through the water of your soul.
River you promised to come back… in silence.
Enlightened perception, my most prized of all possessions.
Make a better tomorrow, by today's progressions.
Embraced by the ethereal essence of you,
I find the shadow of myself again.
We got used to it, the killers also got used to it, they are among us.
All the time. Every day a mother watches the murderer who killed her son.
Free. Anyone can murder. Maybe.
Twenty-four people separated by distance.
Twenty-four souls brought closer together by words.
The sweet promises of your love captured my soul.
Exhilarated by you that brings out the radiance of my being.
Unify the voices of ordinary people and watch.
As a vibrant chorus is born.
The sun touches my soul, I feel the feeling of possibility
We are just custodians of the world, to hand to the next generation better then we found it.
Sleepy sunrises castings shadows upon the land.
Illuminating souls looking to the sky.
In nature, nothing exists alone …
You are my flesh; I am your bone.
The world appears that it is going to fail.
But the people always fight back.

www.ingramcontent.com/pod-product-compliance
Lightning Source LLC
Chambersburg PA
CBHW031236290426
44109CB00012B/319